Selito Meira

Order of Salvation

Selito Meira

Order of Salvation

Twelve Concept

CREDO EDICIONES

Imprint
Any brand names and product names mentioned in this book are subject to trademark, brand or patent protection and are trademarks or registered trademarks of their respective holders. The use of brand names, product names, common names, trade names, product descriptions etc. even without a particular marking in this work is in no way to be construed to mean that such names may be regarded as unrestricted in respect of trademark and brand protection legislation and could thus be used by anyone.

Cover image: www.ingimage.com

Publisher:
CREDO EDICIONES
is a trademark of
International Book Market Service Ltd., member of OmniScriptum Publishing Group
17 Meldrum Street, Beau Bassin 71504, Mauritius
Printed at: see last page
ISBN: 978-613-3-92442-0

INDEX

PRESENTATION

One day, use the church, the number of steps of salvation, in chronological order.
I was looking for theological material to substantiate or intend to practice, I searched, without my collection, on the internet and in bookstores, I found nothing finished.

What I found was material, some with depth and logic, others so carried or name but what content did not have.

So for a year I was taught, gathering material, seeking experiences, learning and teaching, I came to this material that is now present.

I opened to certain approaches and founded even more on my convictions, I hope the help will be of great help, as you see the need as well as small group discipleship, and this is how to synthesize the church that needs today, something in which every concept presented It can be an example of a class, or a theme for a cell meeting.
And certainly one, theme for a cult sermon.

"Live, above all, by the manner worthy of the Gospel of Christ, so that, whether you come to see yourself or be absent, hear, do not touch others, who are firm in spirit, as one soul, fighting for the evangelical faith." . Philippians: 1; 27

SALVATION ORDER

When we enter Christianity, we find it simplified for some. who do not accept criticism or disagreement under the assertion of our faith that blindly must be obeyed and prompt. Yet even within this monotheistic faith that believes in one God. We see distortions and childishness being practiced.

We apparently find an idea of a God who: Creates a man gives him a law called free will, and if he did not correspond to him, he would already show him another project called redemption that would be obtained strictly by Faith.

When we then come across lines of interpretation of the real concept of this faith, questions soon arise, such as why certain liturgies and affirmations of what and what to believe, thinking of this we go into a logical situation:

Is there a chronological or even logical order of this faith?

Then we find four concrete lines that were grounded in the early days of Christianity, which is the ORDER of SALVATI conceptualized and propagated by Roman Catholicism, Lutheranism, Arminianism, and Calvinism.

With different views on the same faith, each doctrinal current claims that its position is the correct one, or at least the most faithful to what the holy scriptures reveal to us, yet right now we are having a hard time with what goes on as theological grounding.

Some put voracious rules making it difficult for people thirsting for salvation, others put ease relativizing this same rule of salvation. But nothing is more logical than observing what sound doctrine tells us.

Regardless of the interpretations one has, the identified chronology is from the CALL by the Lutheran concept. The call can be understood as the presentation of Jesus, his acceptance or conversion. Culminating with GLORIFICATION by the Arminian and Calvinist concepts. That is the final state of the believer in Jesus.

CATHOLICISM

Being the first by the Catholic Church that does not define a single time, the interpretation of the Order of Salvation because it is believed: (Catholics believe that this concept comes straight from the disciples, the main Peter).

MARTIN LUTHER

Martin Luther born November 10, 1483, died February 18, 1546 was a German monk, professor and theologian based on 95 theses (published in 1517) contrary to Catholic clerics. So it was in him that the Protestant reform arises.

JACO ARMINIO

In Latin Jacobus Arminius, of Dutch descent born on October 10, 1560 and died on October 19, 1609 being his real name Jakob Hermanszoon. Theologian of Protestant Reformation times.

JOHN CALVIN

Born on July 10, 1509, died on May 27, 1564, a French theologian, with a strong influence during the Reformation, disliked Luther and Arminius for their strong belief in predestination. It is a passage defended to this day by the followers of his teachings.

This is the position of the concepts described above:

Catholicism:	**Lutheranism:**	**Arminianism:**	**Calvinism:**
BAPTISM	CALL	FOREKNOWLEDGE	PREDESTINATION
CONFIRMATION	ENLIGHTENMENT	PREDESTINATION	ELECTION
EUCHARIST	REPENTANCE	ELECTION	CALL
PENANCE	REGENERATION	PREVENTIVE GRACE	REGENERATION
EXTREME ANOINTING	JUSTIFICATION	EXTERNAL CALL	FAITH
	MYSTIC UNION	REPENTANCE AND FAITH	REPENTANCE
	SANCTIFICATION	REGENERATION	JUSTIFICATION
	CONSERVATION	JUSTIFICATION	SANCTIFICATION
		SANCTIFICATION	PERSEVERANCE
		GLORIFICATION	GLORIFICAÇÃO

We find, in this order, the four positions of the order of salvation, but converging and diverging points in these doctrinal followings, and what else is being accepted in this order is twelve conceptual steps in which for lack of clarity and even the very acceptance of a different doctrinal current as possible is as follows:

- PRESCIENCE
- PREDESTINATION
- CALL
- FAITH
- REPENTANCE
- Justification
- REGENERATION
- ADOPTION
- PERSEVERANCE

Order of salvation O4

- MORTIFICATION
- SANCTIFICATION and
- GLORIFICATION.

Knowing that there is a simplistic action on the part of certain leaders regarding the Ide of Jesus (Matthew 28), we find that for some Christian leaders, who are in the mission field and or in front of churches, such detailed concepts even sound like the beginning of heresy, As far as dogmatic action is concerned, it is true that we do not enter into the legal attitudes of each church, but it is necessary to have a minimum knowledge of what it is going to propagate and its implications in the defense of a faith or doctrine.

“But Jesus answering said unto them, Ye err, not knowing the scriptures, nor the power of God.” Matthew 22:29

"My people are being destroyed because they lack the knowledge ... "Hosea 4:6[a]

When we see a heresy or sect being propagated. A striking feature is the defense of their belief, while in Christianity that this defense should be more fierce we witness certain infantileities promoted by pseudo Christians, contrary to the teachings of the master and apostles.

“But sanctify Christ as Lord in your heart, being always ready to answer everyone who asks you for the hope that is in you.” 1 Peter 3:15

Regardless of the centuries-old conceptual defenses described, we now live what is called the neopentecostal theology.

Also known as the Third Wave of Pentecostalism, it should simply be a junction of the best of Pentecostal and traditional churches, however.

What is more about coming out are violent distortions as to the content of congruent theologies, as a result of neophyte attitudes of leaders trained in this theology, who belittle what was the basis for foreign missionaries who predisposed themselves either by calling or imposing their denominations. come to Brazil to preach the gospel that as a result we have many millions saved. glory to the Father, for I am one of these saved.

So we proceed to the following lines. A little about the doctrine of salvation, far from wanting to give a definitive and absolute concept on each subject approached, because we want to synthesize the dose concepts listed in these pages reiterating that they are information of each concept without pretending to exhaust the subjects as we find scholars and theologians. experienced in some of these themes that would surely embarrass us.

CONCEPT

Certainly our salvation is established by Christ Jesus, his message and vicarious suffering, that is, substitution for ours, and that it must be accepted by faith by grace.

"For by grace ye are saved through faith, and it is not from you; it is the gift of God." Ephesians 2:8

The study of human salvation is called SOTERIOLOGY, a word derived from the junction of two Greek terms; Soterios meaning Salvation and Logos with meaning of word or principle. But I still find Logos as being; Reason, Reason or Idea.

Thus, the plan of salvation is an idea of God, in its smallest detail to lead man to dwell with his creator. So what is human participation in this process?

In Christian theology we have Synergism, the theory that in this salvation the object to be saved, which is man, has participation and is responsible for its salvation or perdition.

Diametrically we have the Monergism, corresponds to the theory that the sole responsibility for the salvation of man is of God, because his decisions are sovereign.

That said, we need to understand what are the quotas of participation in salvation, what is of God and what is of man, so I believe that among the concepts presented we cannot exclude this or that based only on an exposition.

A definition of the Christian doctrine of salvation would be: "The spiritual and eternal deliverance which God immediately grants to those who accept His conditions of repentance and faith in the Lord Jesus." Salvation is possible only through Jesus Christ (John 14: 6; Acts 4:12), and depends on God for his provision, security, and security.

What is certain is that the Father has a project for us all according to the golden text of his love for all who believe.

"For God so loved the world, that he gave his only begotten Son, that whosoever believeth in him should not perish, but have everlasting life. 17 Therefore God sent his Son into the world not to condemn the world, but that the world was saved through him."John 3:16

If God has a plan for human salvation, the rational question is to be saved from what?

- the wrath of God;
- Of impending doom.
- Of eternal suffering.

From God's wrath:

In Adam there was a rupture of the initial plan of the creator, in the couple's breach of obedience in paradise, generating the separation of the creature with the creator. Providing a plan in which divinity itself would promote this reconciliation for free, that is, Christ Jesus, called salvation, yet if the creature did not accept such a plan then it will have to pass a judgment in which God's wrath will manifest. Therefore salvation is the liberation from the consequences of sin, completely removing it from this verdict, removing from us the wrath of God.

"For all have sinned and fall short of the glory of God" Romans 3:23

"For the wages of sin is death ..." Romans 6:23

"Much more then now, being justified by his blood, we shall be saved from wrath through him. 10 For if we, when enemies, were reconciled to God through the death of his Son, much more, being reconciled, we shall be saved through his life." Romans 5:9,10

Of impending doom:

In the first couple's folly, their disobedience led to spiritual death, that is, separation that interrupts the direct relationship with God, then physical degeneration, that is, man's death, physical or corporal death, separating immaterial (spirit) man from material (body).

"And the Lord God gave him this commandment; You shall eat freely from every tree in the garden, 17 but you shall not eat from the tree of the knowledge of good and evil. For in the day that thou eatest thereof thou shalt surely die." Genesis 2:16,17

Consequently in Adam all now born are born one in a state of spiritual death, that is, separated from God, but his great love is manifest:

"For God so loved the world, that he gave his only begotten Son, that whosoever believeth in him should not perish, but have everlasting life. 17 For God sent his Son into the world, not to condemn the world, but to save the world through him. 18 He who believes in him is not condemned; but he that believeth not is condemned already, because he believeth not in the name of the only begotten Son of God." John 3:16,18

Of eternal suffering:

Believing in eternal life, it is evident that our desire is to receive all that the holy scriptures reveal to us as good as eternal life itself in heaven free from any danger and any future suffering is logical. For the word relates that in this suffering the fire is unquenchable.

"And if your hand causes you to stumble, cut it off; for it is better to go into life with one hand than to have both hands, to go into hell, into unquenchable fire 44 where the worm dies not, neither the fire is quenched." Mark 9:43,44.

"And these shall go into everlasting punishment, but the righteous into everlasting life." Matthew 25:46.

"But what does she say? The word is near you; it is in your mouth and in your heart, that is, the word of faith that we are proclaiming: 9 If you confess with your mouth that Jesus is Lord and believe in your heart that God raised Him from the dead, you will be saved. with the heart one believes for righteousness, and with the mouth one confesses for salvation." Romans 10:8,10

Salvation Times

In regard to the time of salvation, both adepts of the doctrine of predestination and those of foreknowledge agree that at the three times of salvation:

- • In Greek, I proorize, previously determined, to predestine, to decide beforehand, predestination is God determining rather the occurrence of certain things.

- Whereas foreknowledge is the foreknowledge of God or foreknowledge, thus associated with the concept of election.

- In the divine attribute, Eusebius Passphil states that:

"Prior knowledge of events is not the cause of their occurrence. Things don't happen just because God knows. When things are about to happen God knows it. "He gives man the possibility to modify his version in the future, but God does not fail to foresee them, but man does not interfere with the sovereign will of the Creator.

In Corinthians we see:

"Yet in ourselves we have had the sentence of death, that we should not trust in ourselves, but in the God who raises the dead 10 who has delivered us and will deliver us from such a great death. whom we have hoped will still continue to free us." II Corinthians 1:9,11

In the past:

In the verb deliver we observe different tenses regarding salvation because in the calling and justification, it is characterized as a finished, complete work, as a determined act:

"Who saved us and called us with a holy vocation; not according to our works, but according to his own determination and grace given to us in Christ Jesus, before the everlasting times." II Timothy 1:9,9

"Who was delivered because of our transgression, and was raised again because of our justification." Romans 4:25.

In the present:

Salvation is as a continuous act, in full development, as a process, directly linked to sanctification.

"So then, my beloved, as you have always obeyed, not only in my presence, but much more now in my absence, develop your salvation with fear and trembling." Philippians 2:12

"Follow peace with all men and holiness, without which no man shall see the Lord." Hebrews: 12:14

Developing in the Philippines has the meaning of continuous work to accomplish or complete something. It is true that mention is made of salvation.

In the future:

At this time all the promises of the Lord concerning salvation are ended, for the events followed are the coming of Jesus, the rapture of the church, the resurrection of the dead, and the possession of eternal life.

"Now we say this to you, by the word of the Lord, that we who live, who remain until the coming of the Lord, will not precede those who sleep. 16 For the Lord himself, having given his commandment, after hearing the voice of the archangel, and the trumpet of God shall sound, shall come down from heaven, and the dead in Christ shall rise first: 17 then we. The living that remain shall be caught up with them among the clouds to meet the Lord in the air, and thus we shall be with the Lord forever." I Thessalonian 4:15,17

Salvation is individual and we have to obtain it in life through our choices and decisions. Once dead, nothing can change the fate we choose in life.

"But as many as received him, to them gave he power to become the sons of God, even to them that believe on his name" John 1:12

"He who believes in the Son has eternal life; but he that rejecteth the Son shall not see life, but the wrath of God abideth upon him." John 3:36

"I assure you, he who hears my word and believes in him who sent me has eternal life and will not be condemned but has passed from death to life." John 5:24

"And this is the testimony: God has given us eternal life, and this life is in his Son. He who has the Son has life; he who does not have the Son of God does not have life. I have written these things to him. you who believe in the name of the Son of God, that you may know that you have eternal life" 1 John 5:11,13

"I am not ashamed of the gospel, for it is the power of God to the salvation of every one that believeth, first of the Jew, after the Greek." Romans 1:16

"For the grace of God has shown salvation to all men. It teaches us to renounce wickedness and worldly passions and to live wisely, justly, and godly in this present age." Titus 2: 11,12

God's will is the salvation of all:

"Who desires all men to be saved and to come to the knowledge of the truth." I Timothy 2:4

To believe in salvation we need to believe in the person of Jesus Christ and his sacrifice, if we reject him we are denying our salvation.

For it is offered to us free of charge and suggests we remain faithful until the end.

"And as men are commanded to die once, after this the judgment cometh, 28 so Christ, having offered himself once for ever to take away the sins of many, shall appear without sin unto the second time. who await him for salvation." Hebrews 9:27,28.

Jesus came to save the world, not to condemn it. God hates sin, but He loves the sinner, and He is sure He will always be willing to forgive Him when He humbles Himself in the presence of the Father by repenting of His evil ways.

"Let the wicked forsake his way, and the man his thoughts; turn to the Lord, who will have pity on him; and to our God, because he is generous in forgiving" Isaiah. 55 7.

Saved, freed from wrath, guilt, condemnation, corruption, and death all by grace! Under the cloak of righteousness, holiness, life, and glory we are led to light, from death to life, from shame to glory, from hell to heaven all by the power of God's wonderful grace! And all because of the eternal, sovereign love of him who has chosen the things that are not to reduce to nothing the things that are, so that no flesh will glory in His presence! Glory to Jesus our Lord, Maranatha!

PRESCIENCE

"For who has known the mind of the Lord to instruct him? I Corinthians 2:16

If there is a divergent concept, these are PRESCIENCE AND PREDESTINATION. Observation is simple all that is instilled for a long time becomes an indisputable law even if the explanations are shallow.
Speaking to a Catholic that he is idolatrous, let's get into a fight, because the concept is not to be idolatrous, but what he does is to worship or is devoted to a saint, where is idolatry, the cult? Similarly, the predestination touted by Luther and Calvin is centennial, (1500) grounded in the word yes, but which calls into question the other concepts with, for example, the Election, when we see assertive discussions to defend this concept, change. the meaning of words and even there is the application of sophistry, which bring down mercy and grace.

"If any man attribute any part of salvation, even the smallest part of it, to man's free will, he knows nothing about grace, and has not known Jesus Christ correctly." M. Luther

Would Luther today bring such a statement?

So just because the word is not widely used does not mean that its concept is not implied.

Foreknowledge In the Aurelius Dictionary: Science of the Future, Knowledge that God has of all that is to come.

Foreknowledge: God's divine attribute to know the future.

In the dictionary Aurelius Predestination is: Belief that each event is determined beforehand by God. Arguing that God would not be the almighty if He did not command it.

Predestination: It is the doctrine that all events have been desired by God.

Free will: that is, free judgment, is the ability of the human will to choose between good and evil, between right and wrong, consciously known.

Within the attribute of omniscience God knows the whole created universe; matter and spirit; in its inconceivable vastness, complexity, the minuteness of its parts, the subtlety of thoughts, the volition. Know both the possible and the real, the future as the present is in its presence,

"You neither heard them, nor knew them, neither were their ears opened beforehand, for I knew that ye would proceed very treacherously, and were called a transgressor from the womb." Isaiah 48:8.

"You know when I sit and when I get up; by far penetrate my thoughts. 3 You search my walk and my bed, and know all my ways. 4 The word has not yet come to my tongue, and you, Lord, know it all." Psalm 139:2,4

"Count the number of the stars by calling them all by their name." Psalm 147:4

As a foreknowledge, in the free actions of men, how can the Lord know the end result and yet not interfere with these actions, if from our birth these actions would be determined by Him?

"Behold, the first predictions have been fulfilled, and I announce new things to you; and before they happen, I will cause them to hear." Isaiah 42:9

"I announce from the beginning what is to happen, and from ancient times, things that have not yet happened; saying, My counsel shall stand, I will do all my will." Isaiah 46:10

The verb "to know" in Greek is ginosko to come to know; know and know. While the Greek term prognosis can be PRESCIENCE, PROVIDENCE AND PREKNOWLEDGE.

"Peter, apostle of Jesus Christ, to the elect who are strangers to the Dispersion at Point, Galatia, Cappadocia, Asia and Bithynia, 2 elected, according to the foreknowledge of God the Father, in sanctification of the Spirit for the obedience and sprinkling of the blood of Jesus Christ. grace and peace be multiplied unto you." I Peter 1:1,2

Elected, in the Greek term, means called, by choice or selection, (Psalm 105: 43), while Foreknowledge is translated as known, associated with the text of Ephesians, "chose us" emphasizes the concept of election, this choice is intended the praise of his glory, and to be made children by adoption, and adoption is yet another concept of salvation.

"As he hath chosen us in him before the foundation of the world to be holy and blameless before him; and in love5 he predestined us to him, for the adoption of children through Jesus Christ, according to the good pleasure of his will, 6 to praise the glory of his grace" Ephesians 1:4,6

Foreknowledge of an act makes it right, but does not compel it. The result is not fatalistic, for if it were so, for example, in the birthright rule we would have Ishmael instead of Isaac, we would have Esau in the place of Jacob and Jonathan in the place of David etc ... Rahab's lie could not be the cause of his salvation, Lot's incest could not result in two nations! God knows them, that is, the laws, and therefore knows beforehand what we will do. However, this still does not solve the whole mystery. But apparently God's omniscience is not causative, it does not produce, just know, even what men in their freedom will choose, despite giving everyone the necessary opportunities for their path so that anyone has to admit his justice. at the trial.

The difficulty today is that if there is foreknowledge, ie foreknowledge, then every human decision or act has already been determined by God, in reality it is not understood how much God interferes with our decisions by relativizing the power of God. , as if He were so busy deciding what to eat and drink or wear tomorrow.

"For those who before knew them also predestined them to be conformed to the image of their Son." Romans 8:29

"God did not reject his people whom he once knew." Romans 11:2

"You, therefore, beloved, knowing this beforehand." 2 Peter 3:17

"Knowing me from the beginning." Acts 26:5

"Which, in fact, was once known, even before the foundation of the world." 1 Peter 1:20

"To him delivered to you by the determined counsel and foreknowledge of God." Acts 2:23

"Elect according to the foreknowledge of God the Father." I Peter 1:2

In the latter, "callings" we see clearly that there being a definite purpose in God for the salvation of man, it is undeniable that foreknowledge is a divine attribute, for if the intention of God's creation was for man to glorify him, to enjoy his communion and live according to your will! Then God's purpose will be fulfilled. For it is written:

"After these things I saw, and behold, a great multitude, which no man could number, from every nation, kindred, people, and tongue, standing before the throne and before the Lamb, clothed in white garments, with palms in their hands." Revelation: 7 ; 9

"Paul, an apostle of Christ Jesus by the will of God" Ephesians 1:1

In John's view, where many are saved, and in Paul's claim to be elected by the Father's will, it would not be light on our part to say that for divine purposes God uses his attributes, for He is Sovereign. Attribute is an immanent quality to its nature, its perfections, its character and nature. In this case above prescience refers to foreknowledge in relation to one of its attributes. With legitimacy to intervene in facts and events, because this has as its final result what was predicted, the consummation of all its promises.

However, when foreknowledge and use as foreknowledge enters the attribute of Omniscience, and we would say that it is foreknowledge, and when used as a divine act, it becomes a doctrine of God's decrees, the knowledge of wholeness. of futuristic futures by human vision, now moving to the sense of foreordination

As far as foreordination or foreknowledge applies to events, including man's free action, it indicates a divine prediction or foreknowledge. When it refers to people, it has a sense of favor, denoting not just an action of the mind, but an affection for a person in view.

"And there is no creature that is not manifested in his presence; on the contrary, all things are discovered and patent in the eyes of those who have been held accountable. "Hebrews: 4; 13

In the verses below, this explanation or verb to know denoting foreknowledge, in relation to the feature. Permissive action, choice and disapproval:

"They made kings, but not for me." Hosea 8:4

"Before you formed in the womb I met you." Jeremiah 1:5

"Of all the families of the earth I have known you only." Amos 3:2

"For the Lord knoweth the way of the righteous." Psalm 1:6

"And then will I profess unto them, I never knew you." Matthew 7:23

"I am the good shepherd, and know my sheep, and am known of mine." John 10:14

"But if anyone loves God, he is known to him." Corinthians 8:3

"The Lord knows those who are his." II Timothy 2:19

Regardless of what our interpretation may be, we err in wanting to place imperative and determining acts on God, whether by foreknowledge or predestination, for we see statements from different texts in which other elements are essential to human salvation, for example:

"Therefore, brethren, seek ever more diligently to confirm your vocation and election; For in so doing you shall not stumble at any time." II Peter 1:10

"Follow peace with all men and holiness, without which no man shall see the Lord" Hebrews 12:14

As for free will, free judgment, interpretation is ambiguous, for I have two ways to choose, yet if I choose the path of life and blessing, my free will ceases to exist as I voluntarily live now for Christ. (Deuteronomy: 30; 15-20.)

If my voluntary choice is not to follow Christ, I will soon be serving the enemy of souls, and many believe they will not be serving anyone, a sad mistake!

"I take heaven and earth today as witnesses against thee, that I set before thee life and death, blessing and cursing; therefore choose life, that you and your seed may live." Deuteronomy 30:19

If we have been elected to salvation and sanctification, Foreknowledge gives us greater scope to develop our salvation and being sanctification a spiritual act, throws us into separation and therefore if we walk in sanctification if the elect or predestined will surely be in the heavenly kingdom to come.

CALL

Interestingly, in the doctrine of Christianity, where we find the so-called Great Commission, Matthew 28: 18-20, the scope of the goal is to reach all nations. The commission obliges us to give a broad exposition of this gospel, but it does not oblige anyone who has contact with it to follow it.

We can understand it this way:

1. In the call one is made aware of the doctrine, and afterward not claim ignorance;

2. In the call one takes knowledge for salvation;

3. In the so-called one becomes aware to be a propagator of Christianity and

4. Another call is the ministerial call.

In the four points above we see them subdivided into two groups which are:

• GENERAL CALL

• EFFECTIVE CALL.

The so-called GENERAL is known as the outer and the so-called EFFECTIVE is known as the inner.

The standardization of the doctrine of salvation has in its beginning the general call of the gospel, which expresses the will and promise of salvation by Jesus Christ, exhortation to repentance, living in this pattern, and blessings that come from this gospel.

"Many are called, but few are chosen." Matthew 22:14

"Many" is part of the general calling, a call to repentance and the faith inherent in this gospel.

In the parable of the sower analogously Jesus presents the heart of man as a field to be sown with different soils. Matthew 13: 1-23 The heart of man is presented in four kinds of soil and only one part really receives all the benefits of the gospel.

No one who has contact with the gospel can claim injustice, for if the gospel was presented the rejection was by will, and its exclusion from the heavenly and perfectly just kingdom.

"The Spirit and the bride say; Comes! Let him that heareth say; Comes! Let him who is thirsty come and whosoever will receive the water of life freely." Revelation 22:17

In the so-called General we can have saved and unsaved people example:

Saves:

- One of the crucified evildoers;

"And he said, Jesus, remember me when thou comest into thy kingdom. 43 Jesus answered and said unto him, Verily I say unto thee, To day shalt thou be with me in paradise." Luke 23:42,43

There was no time for the exposition of the gospel, no baptism, but the Lord's own statement that it would be in paradise, any doubt?

Not saved:

- The rich young man;

"When the young man heard these words, he departed sadly, because he had many properties." Matthew 19:22

In the call of faith this young man was reproved, for his love and keeping the commandments was in love the riches of this world.

Basically in the simple call GENERAL is the presentation of the gospel to all nations.

In the so-called EFFECTIVE, Those who readily respond to this call are the chosen or elect experiencing a supernatural approach to God.

"We know that all things work together for good to them that love God, them that are called according to my purpose." Romans 8:28

In this call the concept of the elect is evident, for the elect or chosen were not only with the exposition of the gospel, but also with the responsibility of the propagation, teaching and defense of this gospel.

"It was not you who chose me; On the contrary, I have chosen you and appointed you to go and bear fruit, and your fruit to remain; that whatsoever ye shall ask the Father in my name, he will give it unto you." John 15:16

When the call has the sense of choice, we see in Exodus the identification, the filling of the spirit, the ability and intelligence given by the Lord, for a specific work, not exempting others with the same aptitude.

"Behold, I have called by name Bezalel the son of Uri, the son of Hur, of the tribe of Judah, 3 and have filled him with the Spirit of God, with skill, understanding, and knowledge in every artifice." Exodus 31:2,3

While in the general call we have an invitation to humanity generating saved and unsaved, in the effective call we have, in the election, a degree of commitment or whatever work I was called, for example:

"Philip, obeying the divine order, from the explanation of the word to the act of baptism, becomes responsible for the arrival of the word in Ethiopia, not for having been there but for practical evangelism with the eunuch." Acts 8:26,40

"The Samaritan woman, the word does not say she became a craft evangelist but her testimony brought salvation to Samaria." John 4:1,42

"Many Samaritans in that city believed him because of the woman's testimony, which he said, He has told me all that I have done." John 4:39

Ultimately we have the effective calling in the vocational sense, the ministry, and the service of the saints in relation to the celestial kingdom. This vocation is not by defining the word as a natural disposition of the spirit or inclination to something.

This call implies the sovereignty of God when He bestows by consent, according to the proportion of Christ's gift to His own for what we call ministerial gifts.

"And he himself gave some to apostles, some to prophets, some to evangelists, and some to

pastors and teachers." Ephesians 4:11

How much of this quote does not make gender distinction, can be male or female.

The sovereign plan of vocation results in holiness imputed by justification and granted by sanctification.

"Do not be ashamed, therefore, of the testimony of our Lord, nor of his imprisonment, that it is I, but share with me the sufferings for the sake of the gospel, according to the power of God, 9 who saved us and called us holy. vocation; not according to our works, but according to his own determination and grace given us in Christ Jesus, before the everlasting times, 10 and now manifested by the appearance of our Savior Christ Jesus, who not only destroyed death, but brought to light life and immortality through the gospel.11 To which I was appointed preacher, apostle, and teacher." II Timothy 1:8,11

Conclusion:

In the general call salvation is the full responsibility of the listener to accept or reject it.

In the effective call responsibility lies in the distinction of vocation.

"For every high priest, being taken in the teeth of men, is constituted in things concerning God, in behalf of men, to offer both gifts and sacrifices for sins, 2 and he is able to pity the ignorant and the erring. he himself is surrounded by weakness.3 And for this reason he must offer sacrifices for the sins of both the people and himself.4 No one therefore takes this honor upon himself except when called by God." Hebrews 5:1,4

FAITH

Faith in literal concept has:

From Latin you are equal to faithfulness;

From the Greek *pistia*: is the firm belief that something is true, without any proof or objective criteria of verification, for the absolute trust we place in this idea or source of transmission.

Accompanied by absolute abstinence from doubt by the inherent antagonism of the nature of these psychological phenomena and conceptual logic. Therefore it is impossible to doubt and have faith at the same time.

Faith manifests itself in many ways and can be linked to emotional issues, such as comfort in times of distress devoid of signs of future improvement, relating to hope, and to motives considered morally noble or strictly personal and selfish. In the religious context faith, even in the literal definition has many meanings. Sometimes it means that someone accepts loyalty to a particular religion based on beliefs or views held to be true.

Faith in the biblical concept:

"Now faith is the assurance of things hoped for, the conviction of things not seen," Hebrews 11:1

Faith is described as the strongest conviction possible, God's present assurance of a future reality.

Faith can be:

• a certainty;

• a trust;

• A belief and

• A gift.

Salvation is indispensable, even if there is no uniformity in the understanding of justification, understood as a juridical act, a substitution of the penalized by Christ.

Justification is by faith:

"Therefore being justified by faith, we have peace with God through our Lord Jesus Christ." Romans 5:1

We also have the ramifications of faith:

- Natural Faith;
- Saving Faith;
- Persevering Faith
- Sanctifying Faith and
- Faith as a gift.

Natural Faith:

I can believe the claim that there is a law, called: Law of Gravity One of the four fundamental forces of nature. But I cannot believe in the creative power of a God who claims to have created you all things.

"By faith we understand that the worlds by the word of God were created; so that which is seen was not made of what is apparent." Hebrews 11:3

Natural faith is believing in the tangible, the visible and not the supernatural.

"Then the other disciples told him; We have seen the Lord. But he answered; If I do not see the sign of the nails in their hands, and there put not my finger, and put my hand on his side, I will not believe." John 20:25

The saving faith:

"And I said to them; Go ye into all the world and preach the gospel to every creature.16 He who believes and is baptized will be saved, and he who does not believe will be condemned." Mark 16:15,16

"For by grace are ye saved through faith; and this does not come from you." Ephesians 2:8

Faith is the "sine qua nom" condition without which there is no salvation.

Saving faith in its composition must have all the information to the concept of this salvation. Personal belief or trust and therefore intellectual assent will help to bring such salvation in a spirit of humility.

"Beloved, when I was diligently writing to you about our common salvation, I felt compelled to correspond with you, urging you to work diligently for the faith once delivered to the saints." Jude 3

"In faith for salvation, faith must be employed in the present tense, "believing" for it is a continual act, a permanent condition for obtaining true righteousness, which proceeds from the gift of God" Ephesians 2:8

Three elements:

1. Intellectual or mental;

We must understand the message of the good news, the truth about Christ.

2. Emotional:

Understanding and accepting the facts with sorrow over sin, and joy over mercy; and

3. Volutive:

Spontaneously submitting to Christ for His will, trust, and hope.

Another faith presented is PERSEVERANT FAITH, must be intense and constant in God.

"Do not, therefore, abandon your confidence; she has a great reward.36 Indeed, you need perseverance, that, having done the will of God, you may obtain the promise. 37 For yet a little while, he that cometh shall come, and shall not tarry; 38 But my righteous shall live by faith."

Hebrews 10:35,38

Therefore it must be a lifestyle.

"Since the righteousness of God is revealed in the gospel, from faith to faith, as it is written: The righteous shall live by faith." Romans 1:17

Faith obeys hierarchy and a logical command:

"But the centurion answered, Lord, I am not worthy that thou shouldest come into my house; but he only commands with one word, and my boy will be healed.9 For I too am a man under authority, I have soldiers at my command, and I say to him; go, and he goes; and to another, come, and he comes; and to my servant, do this, and he does. 10 And when Jesus heard this, he said, And said unto them that followed him, Verily I say unto you, Not even in Israel have I found faith like this." Matthew 8:8,10

In Luke 7 the account of this episode presents more consistent facts about this exercise of faith, because there was the generosity and sympathy of this Centurion towards the Jewish people,

- Friend of the Jews;
- Collaborated with the construction of the synagogue;
- Requested the intervention of the Elders;
- Recognized his unworthiness and
- The request was not for him, but for one of the servants.

Another text that exemplifies faith in the form of authority is the Canaanite woman;

"Then he answered and said, It is not good to take the children's bread, and to cast it to the dogs. 27 But she said, Yes, Lord, but the dogs eat of the crumbs that fall from their owners' table. Then said Jesus unto him; O woman, great is your faith! Do it to yourself as you wish. And from that moment on, her daughter was healthy." Matthew 15:26,28

Sanctifying Faith:

Intrinsically, the development of sanctification is linked to the process of perfecting character and leading the Christian to a state of maturity, for without faith it is impossible to please God.

"Now without faith it is impossible to please him; For he who comes to God must believe that he is, and that he is a rewarder to those who seek him." Hebrews 11:6

"But you, beloved, building up yourselves in your most holy faith, praying in the Holy Spirit." Jude 20.

Faith as a gift:

It is a gift of the Holy Spirit:

"To another faith in the same Spirit" I Corinthians 12:9

In the amplified bible the definition of faith goes like this:

"Now faith is the conviction, the confirmation, the certitude of the things we hope for, the

proof of the things we don't see, and the conviction of their reality. Faith is to perceive as real what is not revealed to the senses." Hebrews 11:1

The gift of faith here is an integral part, the so-called spiritual gifts, so this gift is dimensional, sometimes manifested in conjunction with that of knowledge and science (I Corinthians 12:8).

Dimensional, because it is something that goes beyond the natural, because it creates what does not exist, it is the divine capacity to make his word worth revealing God himself and make him glorified.

The passages which present this dimension to human eyes can be proved only after the events and facts are seen by the witnesses, their agents acting as if they were a demonstration of foreknowledge, an extreme confidence in the Divine;

From the Old Testament an example:

"Answer me, Lord, answer me, that this people may know that you, Lord, are God, and that you have turned their hearts back to you. 38 Then the fire of the Lord fell, and consumed the burnt offering and the wood. and the stones, and the earth, and licked the water that was in the gully. 39 And when all the people saw it, it fell on its face, and said, The Lord is God! The Lord is God!" I Kings 18:37,39

Examples of the new will:

"Jesus said unto him, Did not I say unto thee, If thou believest, thou shalt see the glory of God?" 41 Then they removed the stone. And Jesus lifting up his eyes to heaven said, Father, I thank thee, because thou hast heard me. 42 By the way, I knew that you always hear me, but I spoke because of the multitude present, that they might believe that you sent me. 43 And when he had said this, he cried with a loud voice, Lazarus, come out! 44 And he that was dead came out, having his hands and feet bound with bandages, and his face wrapped neither with handkerchief. Then said Jesus unto them, Untie him, and let him go." John 11:40,44

The object of our faith is:

No doubt the main object of our faith is Christ Jesus, for He is the idea of God, in this we must believe in the writings of Moses, the prophets, the gospels, and the promises:

"Let not your heart be troubled; believe in God, believe also in me." John 14:1

"Until we all come to the unity of faith and the full knowledge of the Son of God, to perfect manhood, to the measure of the stature of the fullness of Christ," Ephesians 4:13

"Let not your heart be troubled; believe in God, believe also in me." John 14:1

"Jesus answered and said unto them, This is the work of God, that ye believe on him that was sent by him." John 6:29

"For if you indeed believed Moses, you would also believe me; because he has written about me." John 5:46

"Believe on the Lord your God. And you will be safe; believe in his prophets and prosper." II Chronicles 20:20b

"Saying; The time is fulfilled, and the kingdom of God is at hand; repent and believe the

gospel." Mark 1:15

"He did not doubt the promise of God through unbelief, 21 being fully convinced that he was mighty to do what he promised." Romans 4:20,21

In Christ faith must be a special ability to truly be representative of the Lord on this earth, and this implies receiving God's righteousness, suffering as a servant, and being productive:

"For it has been given you the grace to suffer for Christ, and not only to believe in him," Philippians 1:29.

"And to be found in him, having no righteousness of his own, which proceedeth from the law, but that which is by faith in Christ, the righteousness that proceedeth from God, based on faith;" Philippians 3:9

"The hand of the Lord was with them, and many believing turned to the Lord." Acts 11:21

"That your faith should not stand in human wisdom, but in the power of God." I Corinthians 2:5

"Simon Peter, the servant and apostle of Jesus Christ, to those who have obtained with us equally precious faith in the righteousness of our God and Savior Jesus Christ." II Peter 1:1

"Remembering before our God and Father the earnestness of your faith, the self-denial of your love, and the steadfastness of your hope in our Lord Jesus Christ," I Thessalonians 1:3

The channels through which our faith comes are the scriptures and its exposition, for by preaching we come to the knowledge of all information, and much more our prayer is needed to overcome adversity, it is always proved by afflictions and the last statement is What is not from faith is sin:

"But these are recorded, that ye may believe that Jesus is the Christ the Son of God, and that believing ye may have life in his name." John 20:31

"And so faith cometh by preaching, and preaching by the word of Christ." Romans 10:17

"And whatsoever ye shall ask in prayer, believing ye shall receive." Matthew 21:22

"And he said unto them, Because of the smallness of your faith. For verily I say unto you, If ye have faith as a grain of mustard seed, ye shall say unto this mountain, Go from hither unto thither, and it shall pass. Nothing will be impossible for you." Matthew 17:20

"In this you may exult, though at present for a short time, if necessary, you will be saddened by various trials, 7 so that once you have confirmed the value of your faith, much more precious than perishable gold, even though it is determined by fire, it may redound. in praise, glory and honor in the revelation of Jesus Christ." I Peter 1:6,7

"But he who has doubts is condemned if he eats, because what he does is not from faith; and all that is not from faith is sin." Romans 14:23

Faith can be represented as weapons and devices of war, both defense and attack, as virtue has to be diligent:

- shield;

"Always embracing the shield of faith, whereby you may erase all the fiery darts of the

Evil One." Ephesians 6:16

- Armor;

  "But let us who are of the day be sober, putting on the breastplate of faith and love, and taking the helmet of hope for salvation." I Thessalonians 5:8

- Victory;

  "For whosoever is born of God overcomes the world; and this is the victory that overcomes the world, our faith." I John 5:4

- Christian virtue;

  "Therefore you, gathering all your diligence, associate virtue with your faith; with virtue, knowledge; with knowledge, self-control; with self-control perseverance; with perseverance, godliness" II Peter 1:5,6

Conclusion:

Faith has the power to convert us to Christ diametrically opposed to what is contrary to the word of God, makes us aware of who God is of who we are and what awaits us as to the exercise of our faith.

"Looking steadfastly to the Author and Finisher of faith, Jesus, who in return for the joy that was set before them, endured the cross, ignoring ignominy, and is seated at the right hand of the throne of God." Hebrews 12:2

REPENTANCE

The concept of repentance in Christian theology relates to the idea of sin.

For biblically we find two groups of people called the RIGHTS, who walk uprightly and IMPIOS, who practice works of wickedness or sin.

According to this concept, the human being repents of his sin when he becomes aware that he has practiced it, recognizes his condition as a sinner and wishes not to make the same mistake.

However, the sinner is not always willing to repent, and he may be going through another process called remorse that has feelings and affinities in feelings resembling repentance. In this sense, repentance is one of the elements of ORDO SALUTIS, so it becomes a necessary condition for human salvation.

Definition:

REPENTANCE: Sincere regret of any act or omission; contrition. Withdrawal of cause made or undertaken.

REMORSE; Restlessness of conscience for guilt or crime committed.

"When Judas, who had betrayed him, saw that Jesus had been condemned, he was taken with remorse and returned to the chief priests and religious leaders the thirty pieces of silver." Matthew 27:3

Remorse is a feeling experienced by those who believe they have committed an action that violates a moral code (personal or otherwise) that they obey.

Remorse is more intense than sadness and implies a long-term state. At the same time it suggests a degree of resignation which gives remorse a certain degree of dignity. In terms of attitude, remorse can be understood as something between the sadness that involves acceptance and the anguish that would involve non-acceptance.

The word remorse has Latin origin, comes from remorsus, past participle of remordere, which means to bite again. It binds, therefore, to tear, attack, satirize, hurt, torture, torment. The very etymology of the word already gives us the idea of how painful this feeling is and the anguish and even the shame that goes with it. This comes from the awareness that we have acted badly. Usually comes with guilt and lamentation.

Remorse is a feeling about past events and attitudes. It is the feeling of what was not to be said, what was not to be done.

When you practice remorse, it does not mean that you will not sin again.

While when there is repentance, the decision is not to sin.

So when a righteous man commits sin, he knows that he must ask for his forgiveness, since the ungodly that his sinful practice is a habit, he is called to repentance.

"If we confess our sins, he is faithful and just to forgive us our sins, and to cleanse us from all unrighteousness." I John 1:9

"But go and learn what it means: I want mercy, not sacrifice. For I have not come to call the righteous, but sinners to repentance." Matthew 9:13

In Greek we find the word "metanoia" derived from meta meaning "after" and "neo" "understand". In the literal is later reflection or change of mind.

Biblically the meaning goes deeper than the presented is also a change of direction, direction and attitude.

BAPTISM OF REPENTANCE

The ministry of John the Baptist is evident at the beginning of the gospels. His mark was the preparation of Christ's way, message of profound change, and baptism of repentance.

The text is:

"He traversed the whole vicinity of the Jordan, preaching baptism of repentance for the remission of sins, 4 as it is written in the book of the words of the prophet Isaiah:

Voice of one crying in the wilderness, Prepare the way of the Lord, make straight his paths." Luke 3:3,4

The baptism that its origin means burial, plunging or immersing is an outward act of an inward transformation is a burial and this involves death, what? Of the old habits.

Luke shows that it was for the remission of sins, we associate it with the book of Leviticus 15, where Moses speaks about the purification of human secretions, literally to cleanse themselves.

So here we see a transition. When John was preaching he was leading the people to acknowledge their sins and publicly expounding through baptism and elevating the meaning of baptism in Christ.

"I baptize you with water for repentance; but he that cometh after me is mightier than I, whose sandals I am not worthy to bear. He will baptize you with the Holy Spirit and with fire." Matthew 3:11

The baptism of repentance was the redirection of the meaning of remission and cleansing from sin, a new positioning of the Jews and Gentiles, moral cleansing, and preparation for the coming of the messiah.

Similar to the concept of Faith, repentance has three phases:

1st Intellectual:

Man without the knowledge of sin has nothing to repent, for the intellectual is responsible for studying speculation about ideas, aware can redirect his life to an assertive action.

When you are exposed to the message of the cross, you become aware that you are a sinner, with no exception, we are called to repentance:

"For all have sinned and fall short of the glory of God" Romans 3:23

"I came not to call the righteous, but sinners, to repentance." Luke 5:32

"Peter answered them; Repent, and each one of you be baptized in the name of Jesus Christ for the remission of your sins, and you will receive the gift of the Holy Ghost." Acts 2:38

2nd Emotional:

Emotional because, it has a cognitive subjective action, subjective referring to the senses inherent to the individual, cognitive, because in the act of knowledge acquisition will have to make a decision regarding their perception, reasoning and judgment.

In emotive action the knowledge of sin generates in us a sadness, having of course a distinction as to the emotions and the result of these emotions:

"I confess my iniquity; I bear sorrow because of my sin." Psalm 38:18

"For godly sorrow produces repentance for salvation, which bringeth no sorrow to anyone;" II Corinthians 7:10

An expression of emotional repositioning with repentance is described in Psalm 51.

3rd Volutive:

Possessing the intellectual and emotional elements, the volitional action that is the individual's ability to choose, their determination must result in a drastic change, because we are instructed in a new posture, there has to be decision making (Luke 15: 17-20); the works of the flesh must be replaced by the fruit of the Spirit (Galatians 5: 19-26) and we become fruitful (Matthew 3; 8, 7, 20)

"Then, falling into himself, he said, How many workers of my father have bread with abundance, I here starve! 18 I will get up and go to my father and say to him, Father, I have sinned against heaven and before you." Luke 15:17,18

"I confessed to you my sin, and my iniquity I no longer hid. Said; I will confess my transgressions to the LORD; and you have forgiven the iniquity of my sin." Psalm 32:5

"Or do you despise the riches of your goodness, your tolerance, and your long-suffering, ignoring that God's goodness leads you to repentance?" Romans 2:4

Works of Repentance:

"God did not take into account the times of ignorance; but now, tell men, that all men will repent everywhere." Acts: 17:30

The imminent eternal death, as a consequence of man's separation from God, can be changed into eternal life with Christ, for reconciliation and subsequent salvation is in the decision not to sin anymore.

The word repent cannot be combined at the same time, it must be a state of constant repentance, it is intrinsic, it is not separate.

It frees you from the past and possible future punishment;

"They were not, I tell you; but if ye do not repent, ye shall all perish." Luke 13:3

Free you from guilt.

"But God proves his own love toward us, that Christ died for us, yet we were sinners." Romans 5:8

Purify you:

"Therefore if any man purify himself from these errors, he shall be a tool of honor, sanctified, and useful to his owner." II Timothy 2:21

The final comparison of the righteous impious verses is described as follows:

"I tell you, thus, there will be greater joy in heaven for a sinner who repents than for ninety-nine righteous who need no repentance." Luke 15:7

This is a good opportunity to bring heaven into a state of celebration: sinners to repentance. Not an invitation is an order!

" Confession of Faith without repentance breeds merely outward devotion";

"Confession of Faith accompanied by repentance generates a life of obedience to God's will."

JUSTIFICATION

The concept of justification is a latent theme in the New Testament, but also existing in the old covenant, which was basically repentance, faith, and bloodshed for atonement, we know that in the old covenant all things converged so that the new covenant would have deepening a supernatural, highlighting the vicarious sacrifice of Christ.
It is the Apostle Paul who gives greater emphasis to the concept of justification.

"But now, without the law, the righteousness of God witnessed by the law and by the prophets is manifested; God's righteousness through faith in Jesus Christ to all who believe; for there is no distinction, 23 for all have sinned and fall short of the glory of God, 24 being justified freely by his grace through the redemption that is in Christ Jesus, 25 whom God hath proposed in his blood as the propitiation through faith. , to manifest his righteousness, because God, in his tolerance, left unpunished sins previously committed; 26 for the manifestation of his righteousness in the present time, to himself be just and the justifier of him that hath faith in Jesus." Romans 3:21,26

Justification is one of the concepts that cannot be dichotomized, for it is a singular but not unique act proceeding from divine grace, but continuous until our complete salvation in Christ.

Therefore, righteousness, justice and justification must be made clear as to its etymology, so:

- FAIR: According to law; to reason, impartial, straight, accurate adjusted and adequate.
- JUSTICE: Compliance with law, fairness, kindness, law and righteousness.
- JUSTIFICATION: Act or effect of justification or justification, discharge of guilt and rehabilitation.

The tripod or method of justification is thus presented: Faith, grace and blood:

Faith; The biblical texts make it clear that justification is by faith:

"Therefore justified by faith we have peace with God through our Lord Jesus Christ." Romans 5:1
"It was not through the law that Abraham or his seed was promised to be heir to the world, but through the righteousness of faith. 14 For if heirs of the law are heirs, faith is broken, and the promise is broken." Romans 4:13,14

Grace: Unmeritorious favor, if there is anything difficult for mankind to comprehend as the grace of God is called grace, for the Father has simply resolved in his heart to be gracious and so is He! Redundancy? But true.
Ephesians in chapter 2 once more the apostle discusses in depth one of the familiar subjects.

"For by grace are ye saved through faith; and it does not come from you; it is the gift of

God." Ephesians 2:8

"Being justified freely by his grace through the redemption that is in Christ Jesus." Romans 3:24

But grace has a price that is paid unilaterally, paid by Jesus:

"For God so loved the world, that he gave his only begotten son, that whosoever believeth in him should not perish, but have everlasting life." John 3:16

Blood; ever present element in the substitution of guilt, the burden of acceptable sacrifices before the Lord in the past, now in Christ is also presented as summary execution and violent death representing the weight of our sins on the cross, promoting remission.

"But God proves his own love for us, that Christ died for us, being us sinners. 9 Therefore, much more now, being justified by his blood, we shall be saved from wrath unto him. 10 For if we, as enemies, were reconciled to God through the death of his Son, much more, being reconciled, we shall be saved through his life." Romans 5:8,10

"In fact, almost everything according to the law is purified with blood; and without shedding of blood there is no remission." Hebrews 9:22

As we have already commented on salvation, it has both individual and collective concepts at the same time.
One completing the other, as to justification it precedes sanctification, so when there is a surrender to Christ saying yes I surrender, faith the grace and mercy of God is manifest;

"Therefore being justified by faith, we have peace with God through our Lord Jesus Christ." Romans 5:1
"And of all things which by the law of Moses ye could not be justified, by him is every man that believeth justified." Acts 13:39

In the concept of justification the natives thus described in the book of Corinthians cannot scale this process, for in the law of the earth the accused is blamed of possible guilt, only after his innocence has been proved, in justification does God clear the guilty by drawing to himself. the penalty of the offense.
We become righteous, not because we deserve it, but because Christ makes us righteous. It is a redemptive work.

"To him that knew no sin he made him sin for us, that we might become the righteousness of God in him." II Corinthians 5:2.

"As it is written: There is not one righteous, not one;" Romans 3:10

"If we confess our sins, he is faithful and just to forgive us our sins, and to cleanse us from all unrighteousness." I John 1:9

In the garden of Eden, by the consummation of sin, human intimacy with God had been compromised, thus promoting God's separation from men resulting in guilt, separation, and condemnation.

Following the acts the Father, in the Person of Moses compiles a law, which if obeyed would bring a certain approximation of God to his own, and to minimize guilt, sacrificial acts were established for the purpose of substituting the blood of guilt animals. of the man.

Transient sacrifice was not enough to erase them.

"In fact, almost everything according to the law is purified with blood; and without shedding of blood there is no remission." Hebrews 9:22

"And it is evident, that by law no man is justified before God: for the righteous shall live by faith." Galatians 3:11

In blame, Forgiveness.

• In guilt, as it refers to personal responsibility that causes moral and spiritual harm, because the conscience is aware of the faults committed before the Creator.

In righteousness, even guilty the Father promotes remission;

"In which we have redemption, the forgiveness of sins" Colossians 1:14

In condemnation, forgiveness.

• In the condemnation, an act of legal impediment to the entrance to heaven and subsequent receipt of the penalty imposed which is eternal imprisonment in the hells, a sentence reserved for unbelievers and sinners,

That in this acquittal there is the practice of forgiveness, an act of mercy of our Lord and savior.

"To the Lord belong mercy and forgiveness" – Daniel 9

In separation, reconciliation.

• In separation, sin has created a barrier between God and men, and the more man sins, the further away he is, where we see marked cruelty, lack of love, unprecedented individualism. Becoming enemies of God.

reconciliation (from Greek Katallassein) shifting from enmity to friendship, the Greek term emphasizes the state to which we find ourselves enemy of God, reconciliation makes us friends of God again promoting a state of peace with God.

"through whom we have received, now reconciliation." Romans 5:11

Justification is a transcendental judicial act, because of course we cannot understand this substitutive act of Christ, which reposition us as to our spiritual state. (John 3:16,21; Romans 4:25). Jesus was justified, punished with the death penalty, (Luke 23:33) took our guilt, even though he was admittedly just (Luke 23:47) justified us, exempted us from guilt,

"Who was delivered because of our transgressions, and was raised again because of our

justification." Romans 4:25

That now in Christ we might be made righteous before God, men, and especially the hosts of wickedness, that we may pray to God the Father and have our prayers answered (Matthew 6:6).

Of men because there is no distinction (Romans: 3:22), of hosts to have authority over them (Luke: 16:17,18)

The justification that is our spiritual situation or position, manifested through faith (Romans 5:1; Acts 13:39), leads us to another concept of the order of salvation which is sanctification:

Sanctification is our spiritual condition, how close we are to God (Hebrews 10:19,25).

"Follow peace with all men and holiness, without which no man shall see the Lord." Hebrews 12:14

In the offense, accused, innocent or guilty, we need a defense, if wrongfully accused proves innocence, if guilty, penalized, only after serving the sentence we are acquitted, we get a clean record! Jesus is this advocate, our advocate,

"But if any man sin, we have an advocate with the Father, Jesus Christ the righteous;" I John 2:1

Fair (Heb.: rect) according to law or law; legal, legitimate, virtuous, in this process we saw that the act of legitimation is by Christ, within his resurrection, has become the pledge of ours, (1 Corinthians 15) so we must undress from every natural attitude, looking at things. from above, which refer to eternity, things which eyes have not seen, have not heard, things which Christ hath prepared for his own (I Corinthians 2:9).

One thing that should be dealt with in the Christian environment is the fact that once we have made the mistake and respectively asked for forgiveness, it is understood that we have been forgiven. Once is not enough, we limit God's mercy when He says that He remembers our sins no more (Isaiah 43:18,19, 25).

Confessing sin, God's faithfulness reaches us, there is a cleansing from unrighteousness, so we become righteous in Christ (I John 1:9), therefore our prayer becomes effective (James 5:16), we understand that In justification, Jesus offering the sacrifice provided us with everything we needed to present to God through our justification!

In the Sermon on the Mount Jesus mentions sunrise and rain as benefits for both the righteous and the wicked (Matthew 5:45), at the present time there seems to be no distinction, but to be justified and to remain righteous implies In many benefits we may find that serving Jesus is painful for us now, Asaph in his psalm (73) observes the prosperity of the wicked and begins to be jealous when he realizes the benefits of doing good, he said: I was brutally acting like an irrational (Psalm 73), Malachi shows a stark difference between righteous and wicked, just for the Lord is like, a private treasure kept, this will be spared by God Himself (Malachi 3:13,18).

To be taken by the Spirit of death to the righteous is to be led to paradise (Luke 23:43), called Abraham's bosom (Luke 16:19,31) for the wicked suffering.

In the rapture of the church is to rise before the great tribulation, is to receive a glorious body (I Corinthians 15:50,58), to the righteous is to build on the foundation of Christ, during his life and service, upon arrival before the court of Christ, there the difference will manifest itself with its respective reward.

"For we must all appear before the judgment seat of Christ, that each one may receive according to the good or evil that he has done through the body" (2 Corinthians 5: 10).

I look at the joy that an athlete expresses when receiving a medal, to a team when being champion receiving the cup. To be righteous after the tribunal is to receive the prepared crowns, which are the crowns of joy, righteousness, life, and glory. Maranata!

"Who was delivered for our sins, and was raised again for our justification." Romans 4:24

"And the gift was not like the offense, for one who sinned. For the judgment came from one offense, indeed, to condemnation, but the free gift came from many offenses to justification." Romans 5:16

"For as by one offense judgment came upon all men to condemnation, so by one act of righteousness grace came upon all men to justify their lives." Romans 5:18

"In justifying sinners God calls them righteous when they really are not; stop imputing to them the sins they have and impute to them righteousness that they don't have." Arthur Tappan Pierson.

REGENERATION

We are talking about concepts that encompass the order of salvation, and of course Regeneration also has its peculiarities as to its definition:

Literal:

1) Regenerate or regenerate action or effect. Reform to improve; Moral renewal.

2) reconstitution of a destroyed or ruined organ;

3) Operation consisting in restoring the activity of a catalyst.

Spiritual:

Revival, moral rehabilitation; reformation of customs, new spiritual life given by baptism and sanctification, rebirth.

In Christian theology regeneration is monergistic: that is, entirely the work of God the Holy Spirit. It raises the elect from the spiritually dead to a new life in Christ (Ephesians 2:1,10). Regeneration is a transition from spiritual death to spiritual life, and a conscious, intentional, and active faith in Christ. It is from the forewarning grace that precedes the proceeding of our hearts to the Lord, in this is its immediate fruit.

"He hath given us life, being ye dead in your trespasses and sins" Ephesians 21

Nicodemus, a fearful and wise man, addresses Jesus on this subject, which not only for him but for many today is also too complex.

"Jesus answered and said unto him, Verily, verily, I say unto you, Except a man be born again, he cannot see the kingdom of God.4 Nicodemus said unto him, How can a man be born when he is old? Can it return to its womb and be born a second time? 5 Jesus answered him; Verily, verily, I say unto you; Those who are not born of water and the Spirit cannot enter the kingdom of God. 6 What is born of flesh is flesh; and he that is born of the Spirit is spirit. you must be born again." John 3:3,7

So how do you put a new man inside an old man? Baptism, repentance, and acceptance begin to demonstrate how this is possible.

Heart and our nature were born again, eyes and ears opened to the truth of this salvation. Cognitive actions have not been removed, we are still what we were.

What happens is a catalyst action, a boosting of the power of God through the Holy Spirit in our lives.

Our sinful and corrupt nature whose root is sin is removed in Christ, but we are not sinless beings, for this is a process already described by sanctification. Act on and on until Christ returns.

The treatises of systematic theology define regeneration as:

Regeneration is a secret act of God by which He gives us new spiritual life.

Also called "born again." John 3:3,8

Looking like a born again, we observe a metamorphosis because the first individual does not cease to exist but is placed purely spiritual elements, in this now regenerated, is the act of God to rule this soul, is the communication of divine life, promoting a New nature. A spiritual resurrection, the promotion of rapprochement with the Creator.

"And so. If anyone is in Christ, he is a new creature. the old things are passed away; behold, they are made new." II Corinthians 5:17

Regeneration project of God.

Historically, at the time of the fall of man, the Lord had already thought of the process of regeneration as may be observed in the law and the prophets, for the Father promises an intervention as to the distant heart of Him, unable to honor Him.

"The Lord your God will surround your heart and the heart of your offspring, to love the Lord your God with all your heart and with all your soul, that you may live." Deuteronomy 30:6

"I will give them one heart, and I will put a new spirit into them; I will take the heart of stone out of their flesh and give them a heart of flesh." Ezekiel 11:19

The above texts show a direct intervention of God regarding the flesh, when added to Joel's prophecy we see complete work: body, soul and spirit.

"And it shall come to pass afterward, that I will pour out my Spirit upon all flesh; your sons and your daughters shall prophesy your old men shall dream, and your young men shall see visions; 29 I will pour out my spirit on those men and women-servants in those days." Joel 2: 28,29

New Testament

The set of factors of the New Testament shows the figure of Christ as its greatest protagonist, because through Him and in Him we are saved.

If we say that regeneration is only by the act of baptism as it is presented to Nicodemus, how then does the Holy Spirit's descent into those of the house of Cornelius?

We then understand that regeneration has a yes sign, but that it is timeless, for some are baptized in water for regeneration, others are baptized by the spirit to then go to the waters.

"Peter still spoke these things when the Holy Spirit fell upon all who heard the word.45 And the faithful of the circumcision who came with Peter wondered, because the gift of the Holy Ghost was also poured out upon the Gentiles; 46 For they heard them speaking in tongues and thanking God. Then said Peter, 47 Can any man refuse water, that these should not be baptized,

which as we have received the Holy Ghost?" Acts 10:44,47

The process itself in the New Testament shows evident acts of regeneration as baptisms in the waters and the Spirit. However, the actual meaning of creation also has the action of regenerating, doing again, and generating.

Thus regeneration aims to radically change our character, promoting knowledge and growth in a God who is pure and holy.

"But what, to me, was profit, I considered loss because of Christ. Yes indeed I regard everything as loss because of the sublimity of the knowledge of Christ Jesus my Lord; For whose sake I have lost all things, and I consider them to be a refuse, to gain Christ, and to be found in him, having no self-righteousness, which proceed from the law, but by faith in Christ, the righteousness that proceed from God. , based on faith; 10 to know him, and the power of his resurrection, and the fellowship of his sufferings, to be content with him in his death;" Philippians 3:7,10

The Need for Regeneration

The need arises for the insertion of the figure of Christ, after the new birth to the individual, this insertion as we have already seen may be by the acceptance of Christ by the Arminian concept or by the election Calvinist concept, act of baptism either by water or by the Holy Spirit.

Once dead in our crimes and sins, now quickened by the regenerating power of the Father.

Thus in the plan of salvation, as receiving agents, as we receive and as spreading agents of this plan regeneration promotes an inclusive action in our lives which is:

Christ as lord of our lives;

Regenerating action of our spirit;

The power of the Holy Spirit and

Spiritual and ministerial gifts.

"But you are not in the flesh, but in the Spirit, if indeed the Spirit of God dwells in you. And if any man have not the Spirit of Christ, he is not his." Romans 8:9

"So consider yourselves also to be dead to sin, but alive to God in Christ Jesus our Lord. Therefore sin not reign in your mortal bodies, but present them to God as instruments of righteousness." Romans 6:11,14

Aspects of Regeneration

Only the divine nature can generate in man a spiritual nature, so when man decides for Christ, his gospel will promote regeneration in the whole man.

Regeneration is a divine act received by those who believe because no one can regenerate himself. Its life-giving agent is the Holy Spirit.

"It is the spirit that gives life; the flesh profits nothing; the words that I have spoken to you are spirit and life." John 6:63

Regeneration gives us an ability to receive new awareness, new thoughts.

"Now we have not received the spirit of the world, but the Spirit that comes from God, that we may know what God has freely given us." I Corinthians 2:12

Regeneration is a supernatural and instantaneous work of the Holy Spirit which gives us the divine life.

"Not by works of righteousness which we have done, but according to his mercy, he has saved us through the regenerating and renewing washing of the Holy Ghost." Titus 3:5

Regeneration is implied in conversion and new birth, for without conversion there is no new birth and without new birth there is no regeneration.

"Blessed is the God and Father of our Lord Jesus Christ, who, according to his great mercy, has regenerated us into living hope through the resurrection of Jesus Christ to the dead." I Peter 1:3

"For ye were regenerated, not of corruptible seed, but of incorruptible, by the word of God which liveth and abide." I Peter 1:23

That said, we see that heavenly tri-unity promotes regeneration for free through the simple exercise of faith, but it is synergistic of God's will, whether by election or conversion within the new birth.

It is God recreating an existing being, implanting in man a desire for his kingdom, empowering him for salvation, energizing him according to the gospel of Christ.

ADOPTION

A testimony:

I am born within the legality of marriage, my masculinity was affirmed by the constant presence of my father, my maternal grandfather and my uncles, always present, and a long time later, when I started working with inner healing and encounters with God that I went to observe the damage. which is made in a life that was begotten, or lives in orphanhood.

So in contact with this kind of concept, called ADOPTION, I hope to somehow help readers understand whether you have never been through this situation so that you can bring understanding of how much suffering is generated in an orphaned soul and those under it. a spirit of orphanhood, of which God is a FATHER and is ready to make us his children.

Our natural relationships can guide our relationship with one of the trinity people to whom we will cling the most, not a rule but, example:

I have good relationship with my father, he was present, affectionate, promoted security, only I have difficulties with friendships;

So I recognize the figure of God as an unreserved father, I will have no difficulty as God's fatherhood over my life.

But the likelihood of my relationship being more intense with the figure of Jesus is great because he is a son and so I will use this relationship to make him my friend.

Who do you have the most relationship with, Father, Son or Holy Spirit?

Adoption means: Action or effect of adopting; Legal acceptance as a child; Tillering, Acceptance and Admission.

In Greek, adoption originates from two words, which together means a placement in sonship: (Huiothesía) HUIOS (son) and (THESIS) a placement.

Adoption indicates in the Greek a juridical term, where God the Father brings us down from his fatherhood, which is the adoption promoted by him, that we are introduced into his great family legally, and as children we have all the rights and privileges that A son has.

In a natural adoption, a person or couple who receives someone as a child confers all the privileges of a natural child. In God we are adopted when we receive the only begotten of the Father, so justification and regeneration also are unique and instantaneous when adopted. confessed to Jesus as our only and sufficient Savior.

"But as many as received him, to them gave he power to become the sons of God: believe them in his name." John 1:12

"See how great love the Father has given us, to the point that we are called children of God" 1 John 3:1

"For ye are all children of God through faith in Christ Jesus" Galatians 3:26

Adoption and justification are equivalent to the grace of the Father, for a judge may acquit wholly one who is being charged with crime, but he may not confer on the acquittal any of the privileges a child has. But the believer in Jesus Christ has the privilege of being able to regard God not only as a judge and justifier, but as a loving father with whom he reconciles.

"But I said, How shall I put thee among the children, and give thee the desirable land, the

excellent inheritance of the armies of the nations? And I said, Father, thou shalt call me, and turn me not astray." Jeremiah 3:19

"To redeem them that were under the law, that we might receive the adoption of children." Galatians 4:5

Adoption and regeneration or new birth are realities that together reveal our assured paternity in Christ. As children, adoption fosters a new relationship, while in regeneration our moral nature changes.

"But as many as received him, to them gave he power to become the sons of God: they believe in his name.13 who were born not of blood, nor of the will of the flesh, nor of the will of man, but of God." John 1:12,13

If a child is adopted when he is born and receives some kind of rejection, whether justified or not, then a person assumes paternity legally, whereas a child born of his own seed cannot be adopted. And son!.

The goodness and love of God reaches us, so much so that when He receives us through the new birth, we are now born as His children, included in His nature.

"For all who are led by the Spirit of God are children of God. 15 For ye have not received the spirit of bondage to live in fear again, but ye have received the spirit of adoption, according to which we cry, Abba Father. 16 The Spirit Himself testifies with our spirit that we are the children of God." Romans 8:14,16

"By whom their precious and great promises have been given to us, that through them you may become partakers of the divine nature, freeing you from the corruption of the passions that are in the world," 2 Peter 1:4

"For they corrected us for a short time, as it seemed best to them; But God disciplines us to profit, that we may be partakers of his holiness." Hebrews 12:10

Old Testament Adoption

A highlighted situation in the Old Testament is that apparently adoption in daughter weighed heavily on the father or patriarch figure, but if the adoptee appears before the firstborn he did not inherit the birthright, slave-born children would count as their mistress's sons and daughters. not of the handmaid, grandchildren born of their children were also adopted as their own, basic texts Genesis 15:2,4; 30:1,26; 48:11,16.

Two striking adoptions in the Old Testament are those of Moses and Esther among several cited;

Moses, if there was no direct intervention of God in his life, in the adoption regime practiced at that time by Egyptian law could make Moses a Pharaoh (Exodus 2: 1-10).

Esther who was made queen for the divine purpose of delivering her people (Esther 2:1,20).

New Testament Adoption

We understand that to be a child of God we must be adopted by Him, as it is the recurring concept, curiously the adoption, first presented in the New Testament is that of his own son, "JESUS". (Matthew 1:18,25):

"And the Holy Spirit descended upon him in the form of a dove; And a voice came from heaven, You are my beloved son; I am well pleased with you. 23And Jesus was about thirty years old when he began his ministry. It was as he cared for, son of Joseph, son of Eli" Luke 3:22,23

"Is not this the carpenter's son?" Matthew 13:55a

Thus from Matthew to Revelation the theme adoption or sonship is found, but the Apostle Paul in much of his teachings treats adoption much more as a legal term of law initiated by justification. Whereas the Apostle John treats the term adoption more as an action of affection, since it always refers to beloved children.

Paul shows us where we are after our adoption and our rights.

"To redeem those under the law, that we might receive the adoption of a son. 6 And because you are sons, God has sent into our hearts the Spirit of his Son, who cries, "Abba, Father! 7 so that you are no longer a slave, but a son; and being a son, also an heir of God." Galatians 4:5,7

John shows Jesus also in a nice but loving way.

"My little children, these things I write to you so that you may not sin. But if any man sin, we have an advocate with the Father, Jesus Christ the righteous; 2 and he is the propitiation for our sins, and not for our sins only, but also for the sins of the whole world." I John 2:1,2

The Apostle Paul, introducing adoption as necessary, to get out of the regime of slavery, mentions adoption as belonging to the Israelites because they are chosen, not in the sense that all born Jews receive salvation, but by God's covenant with them.

"They are Israelites. The adoption, as well as the glory, the covenants, the law, the worship, and the promises belong to them." Romans 9:4

"So you are no longer a slave, but a son; and being a son, heir also of God." Galatians 4:7

"And deliver all who through the dread of death were subject to slavery all their lives." Hebrews 2:15

The servant or slave adoption relationship with his masters in Pauline times was that of an adult, of good character, who had the confidence of his master, but the Apostle shows that God came not only to adopt the good but also the evil and sinners, who in the act of the new birth would have their character regenerated.

Adoption as God's will

We have difficulties, in divine understanding and purposes, so there are various theological currents, be it election, predestination and others, but Apostle Paul in his letter to the Ephesians argues that adoption was already prepared from the foundation of the world, so as situate in time and space something that is in God's sovereignty.

The timeless position places us as adopted children in the present, something prepared even before our existence, an inscrutable situation, because it belongs to the Father! In full exercise of their sovereignty.

"As he hath chosen us in him before the foundation of the world, to be holy and blameless before him, and in love 5 he predestined us to him, to adopt children through Jesus Christ, according to the good pleasure of his will, 6 to praise the glory of his grace, which he has freely bestowed upon us in the beloved." Ephesians 1:4,6

Implications, Benefits and Evidence of Adoption

A very strong sophistry in Brazil, because it is Christianized is that every human being and child of God, we see many sinners ask for God's protection in illicit acts, thinking that the Father brings protection in deception. The bible is very clear about sonship, for only the son of God has Jesus as Lord.

Soon our sonship is confirmed by our conduct, as well as claiming that everyone is a child of God if his own son, Jesus bluntly shows something different?

"You are of the devil who is your father, and you want to fulfill his desires. He was a murderer from the beginning and was never grounded in the truth, because there is no truth in him. When he utters a lie, he speaks his own things, because he is a liar and the father of lies." John 8, 44

The human being without Jesus is a mere creature, and what is in store for them is not pleasant at all.

"But as many as received him, to them gave he power to become the sons of God, even to them that believe on his name: 13 who were not born of blood, nor of the will of the flesh, nor of the will of man. but of God." John 1:12,13

In adoption we receive the love of the Father:

"As a father pities his children, so the Lord pities those who fear him." Psalm 103:13

"But if you who are evil know how to give good gifts to your children, how much more will your Father in heaven give good things to those who ask him?" Matthew 7:1

"Your heavenly Father knows that you need them all." Matthew: 6:32

"But you have received the spirit of adoption, based on which we cry, Abba, Father." Romans 8:15

"I go up to my Father and your Father" John 20:17

We received discipline:

To this day, which is created in Brazilian law, a veto about the correction of children using some way to beat them, either with a spanking or stick, walking against the bible.

"Do not withdraw discipline from the child, for if you beat him with the rod, he will not die." Proverbs 23:13

Due to this lack of correction, we have within the churches people with serious difficulties to accept divine correction, because God is love yes !!! But it is also justice. And if we need to go through corrective acts, Heavenly Father will:

"The Lord correct him whom he love, and beneath every son whom he receive" Hebrews 12:6

"In addition, we had our parents after the flesh, who corrected us, and respected them; shall we not be in much greater submission to the Father of spirits, and then shall we live?" Hebrews 12:9

"For they corrected us for a short time, as it seemed best to them; But God disciplines us to profit, that we may be partakers of his holiness" Hebrews 12:9,10

As a son we receive an inheritance, a kingdom, for we are consistent with Christ, we will have a new body, a new family, which in turn also implies obligations as members of this new family:

"Now if we are children, we are also heirs, heirs of God, and co-workers with Christ" Romans 8:17

"The victor shall inherit these things" Revelation 21:7

"Let these things be present, and things that are to come, all are yours, and yours of Christ, and Christ of God," I Corinthians 3:22

"Fear not, O little flock; for your Father was pleased to give you his kingdom" Luke 12:32

"Come, blessed of my Father! enter into the possession of the kingdom that is prepared for you..."Matthew 25:34

"...We who have the firstfruits of the Spirit, we also groan within ourselves, awaiting the adoption of children, the redemption of our body... the earnest expectation of creation awaits the revelation of the children of God" Romans 8:23,19

"Beloved, we are now children of God, and we have not yet manifested what we shall be. We know that when he appears, we will be like him, because we will see him as he is" 1 John 3:2

As children, we must inherit the name of our father, so it weighs on all God's adopters to represent him as legitimate children in Jesus Christ.

PERSEVERANCE

Looking at the concepts already described, such as justification, regeneration, or adoption among others, we always see God's sharing with man in greater or lesser degree of participation where man opens the heart and the intellect, thus compacting the concepts described above, but in concept of perseverance, we find something only of man even if the trinity is present, for perseverance is a continuous act exercised almost always in distressing moments.

In order to forge character, faith and constancy, always producing hope.

Perseverance:

1) Character or particularity of those who persevere; constancy and persistence;
2) Firmness, constancy in faith, in virtues.
3) Persevere: Persist; keep steady and steady.

When Paul talks about perseverance, he teaches us that it is produced from, or has its origin in tribulation, with sense of extreme pressure, natural persecution and especially spiritual persecution with inevitable problems for the followers of Christ. Generating experience and hope.

If perseverance comes from tribulation, what is tribulation?

We see expressions like; I am passing through the valley, I am in the desert, I am being persecuted, my life is troubled, But what the tribulation has to do with all this!

Tribulation comes from TRIBULUM, which can be:
A threshing instrument;
An instrument that serves to plow the earth.
Tribulum is always associated with land harvest and seeds.

The term tribulation or affliction is linked to a treatment process that God uses to work primarily on the believer's character and faithfulness.

The bible mentions the wheat, as much as its sowing process harvest and result, to plant, one has to clear the ground rip the ground so that the seed penetrates the soil, then there must be the death of the seed, which germinates produce the expected fruit, harvested the grains it has to pass through the mill and after mixing and kneaded, it is taken to the fire to then have the expected result that is the bread.

Therefore tribulation has to be seen as coming from God not for a mere distressing moment, but for building our character and faithfulness.

Tribulation is not punitive action for our sins, but sufferings from situations we do not create, but it is so intense that it is compared to labor pains.

It has to be constructive and not fatalistic. When we see passages as a parable of the sower (Matthew 13) the teaching shows quality of ground and seed, in this we observe, the better the soil treatment and the quality of the seed the result will be excellent.

"Blessed are you when they reproach you for my sake, and persecute you, and in lying speak evil against you. 12 Rejoice and be glad, for your reward is great in heaven. for thus they persecuted the prophets who lived before you." Matthew 5:11,12

"Strengthening the soul of the disciples, urging them to stand firm in the faith; and showing that through many tribulations we are to enter into the kingdom of God." Acts 14:22

We need to introspect, to know if we are being troubled, or if it is simply a consequence of our sins.

Because tribulation is an experience produced by persecution, imprisonment, mockery, poverty, disease, distress, spiritual conflict, and depressive feelings.
It may be the correction of the Father, producing discipline.

"Not only that, but we also glory in our own tribulations, knowing that tribulation produces perseverance, 4 and perseverance experience; and experience, hope." Romans 5:3,4

The tribulations must be momentary, objective and progressive.

"I have told you these things that you may have peace in me. In the world you are afflicted; but be of good cheer; I have conquered the world." John 16:33

"Rejoice in hope, be patient in tribulation, in prayer, enduring," Romans 12:12

As pilgrims on earth, at any given time the tribulation is certain, as are the promises of victory.

"My persecutions and sufferings, which happened to me in Antioch, Iconium and Lystra, what various persecutions I have endured! But the Lord has delivered me from them all.12 Now as many as will live godly in Christ Jesus shall be persecuted." II Timothy 3:11,12

Therefore perseverance is an essential part of the afflicted person's life, as tribulation constantly followed by perseverance generates a state of conquest and victory.

"How great is my frankness to you, and I greatly glory in your cause; I am greatly comforted and overflowing with joy in all our tribulation." II Corinthians 7:4

Perseverance refers to tolerance and ability to remain under trial or pressure without succumbing, bringing an approved character to experience.

So the antonym of perseverance is: inconstancy, impersistence and giving up.

"Do not suppose this man who had attained anything from the Lord; 8 a double minded man, fickle in all his ways." James 1:7,8

Unlike a persevering person, we also have a stubborn, stubborn person who is disqualified by the word, which in its tenacity equates with the sin of idolatry;

"For rebellion is as the sin of witchcraft, and stubbornness is as idolatry and idol worship of the household" I Samuel 15:23

In the early church, which is central to the present-day example of us, it shows that the tripod of perseverance was in sound doctrine in communion and prayer;

"And they persevered in the apostles' doctrine and fellowship, in breaking bread, and in prayers." Acts 2:42

DOCTRINE; The purpose of indoctrination is to impart knowledge, teaching, and discipline.

The apostles' doctrine is based on the truth revealed by God, conveying the fundamental content for the spiritual and relational growth of the church.

"All Scripture is inspired of God and useful for teaching, rebuking, correcting, and teaching in righteousness, 17 that the man of God may be perfectly and perfectly qualified for every good work." 2 Timothy 3:16,17

"So that we may no longer be like boys, shaken from side to side and carried around by every wind of doctrine, by the craft of men, by the cunning with which they lead to error." Ephesians 4:14

"For you say, My doctrine is pure, and I am clean in your eyes." Job 11:4

The logic is in how much knowledge I have of my God and in his teachings, that indoctrinated, we will have a smaller margin of error, in contrast the judgment of this same Lord will be more severe.

COMMUNION: Common union, common participation, and beliefs and ideas, as the communion of the church makes mention of the Holy Supper, when we participate in the Lord's Supper we show that we are in vertical communion, that is we are in communion with the trinity and also the horizontal communion we are in communion with the ecclesia the body of Christ on earth.

Communion is the partnership or sharing among Christians, generated by the unity of the Spirit. Union that is granted to true Christians.

"I beg you, the prisoner in the Lord, to walk worthy of the calling to which you have been called, 2 with all humility and meekness, with longsuffering, enduring one another in love, 3 diligently endeavoring to preserve the unity of the Spirit in the bond of peace;"Ephesians 4:1,3

Communion is Christ-centered, where the most experienced believers support or help those in difficulty.

"Is not the cup of blessing which we bless, the communion of the blood of Christ? Is not the bread which we break, but the fellowship of the body of Christ?" I Corinthians 10:16

PRAYER: Prayer, in Christian belief, is communication and the conscious fruit of a relationship with God during which a person praises, thanks, intercedes for another's life, asks for blessings from him or another, and through him can enjoy the presence. God's.
Prayers are addressed Always and only to God, in the Name of the Lord Jesus who is the ONLY Mediator between God and men; and can be done aloud, spoken, in song, or in silence.

The purpose of prayer (Matthew 6:5,13) would not be to alter God's will, but to obtain for himself and / or the other blessings and graces that God has already bestowed through the Lord Jesus Christ on the Cross.

While in prayer acts and one of the points of perseverance, in Romans Apostle Paul treats prayer as requiring perseverance in an attitude of persistence and regularity.

"Rejoice in hope, be patient in tribulation, in prayer, enduring," Romans 12:12

"Pray without ceasing." I Thessalonians 5:17

PERSEVERANCE, continuous action to stand firm and constant, as part of the order of salvation, the fundamental purpose of salvation is to bring the individual to salvation, because it is situated between the process of adoption, walks through sanctification until glorification.

"It is in your endurance that you will gain your soul." Luke 21:19

And perseverance generates in us a spirit of joy and joy in affirmation as the Apostle James says:

"Behold, we are happy for those who stand firm. Ye have heard of the patience of Job, and have seen the end of the LORD. for the Lord is full of tender mercy and compassion." James 5:11

I see very carefully how the gospel has been spreading, because a gospel of ease is being sold, they are only showing the romantic side without teaching or guiding that in the last days will be difficult days, because it is certain that misleading, false doctrines will appear iniquity. will multiply, there will be great pressure for all to deny their faith.

In the love and consistency of our Father, we receive tribulation and distressing moments, so that we may be found as the purest and most valuable metal.

"Behold, I have honored you, but it has not resulted in silver; I have tested you in the furnace of affliction." Isaiah 48:10

"Do not fear the things you have to suffer. Behold, the devil is about to cast some of you

into prison, to be tested, and ye shall have tribulation ten days. Be faithful unto death, and I will give you the crown of life." Revelation: 2:10

Thus in perseverance, after tribulation, experiences and hope will be reckoned as advancing in the salvation proposed in Christ Jesus, for He is the proof of our perseverance.

MORTIFICATION

When we come to Christ, the command is to be born again, to a new life, when we speak of mortification, it sounds like amphibological, this with more than one interpretation, because how to be born again and live in a state of mortification?
The clear situation is that when we are born again it is for life in the Spirit, while mortifying is to succumb all the desires of the flesh that go against the spirit.

In mortification we find:

1-Act or effect of mortifying.
2-Affliction, torment.
3-Domain, repression of certain senses.
4-Penance that Christians do, to temper the lower appetites and bodily senses, according to the dictates of reason and faith.

MORTIFY: Dull, suppress, or extinguish the vitality, vigor of.

"For we who live are always put to death for Jesus' sake, that the life of Jesus may also be manifest in our mortal flesh." II Corinthians 4:10

"Therefore, brethren, we are debtors, not to the flesh as if constrained to live after the flesh. 13 For if you live according to the flesh, you walk to death. but if by the spirit you mortify the deeds of the body, you will surely live." Romans 8:12,13

"Therefore let your earthly nature die" Colossians 3:5

The Father does not depersonalize us, so the natural senses of the human being remain active. What obliges us as a Christian to live under a new principle of righteousness, we must now be controlled by the Holy Spirit, while the flesh will do its own thing always presenting the delights of sin, but if we decline to its desires we will surely die.

"For if you live according to the flesh, you walk to death; but if by the spirit you mortify the deeds of the body, you will surely live." Romans 8:13

If we want to live in newness of life, the order is to be guided by the Holy Spirit.

"For all who are led by the Spirit of God are the son of God." Romans 8:14

It is imperative, as proof of our salvation, we must treat our sinful flesh as an enemy to be overcome, must express the repudiation of sin severely, for Jesus even constrains us to mutilate ourselves away from any possibility of going to dwell in hell. for it is prepared for the devil and his followers and not for the children of God.
"If your right eye causes you to stumble, pluck it out and throw it from you; for it is fitting for you to lose one of your members, and not let your whole body be cast into hell. And if your right hand causes you to stumble, cut it off from you; for it is fitting for you to lose one of your members, and not let your whole body go to hell" Matthew 5:29,30

We know that many people today flog themselves, whipping or binding themselves to a cross, as if this expression of Jesus were to be observed literally, for it is not today that people seek their own merits for mortification.

One of the exponents of this achievement was the theologian Origines who emasculated himself by literally following this title.

Jesus' direction was not self-mutilation but mortification of the effects of the body, because many interpret that if we now live under grace and not the law we will be treated with different weights, but we observe a grievance regarding the practice of sin in the form of the law. adultery was punished when caught in the act, while in grace if we look with impure intent we already commit adultery!

Mortification by John Owen is:

“The flesh with its faculties and properties, wisdom, cunning, subtlety, strength, must, according to the apostle, be dead, afflicted, mortified — that is, to have its power, life, vigor, and strength to produce its effects, removed by the Spirit. "

The term mortification we may find once or twice in the bible depends on the translation, for mortification is translated as dying, mortifying, torment and affliction, in the present indicative, I mortify; present connective, that I mortify in the affirmative imperative, mortifies you; Perfect in the indicative, I mortified and infinitely personal, for mortifying me (Colossians 3; 5). That put mortification is linear sanctification, without mortification there is no sanctification.

“Always bearing in the body the death of Jesus, so that his life may also be manifested in our body.11 For we who live are always put to death because of Jesus, so that the life of Jesus may also be manifested in our lives. mortal flesh.” II Corinthians 4:10,11

The inexhaustible meaning of the Christian's redemption, which is assured to him, the acceptance by Christ, and that the resurrection is certain, Thus we are made a new creature (II Corinthians 5:17), yet this same Apostle points out that the old man has not ceased to exist, that he is just numb.

Old here is not advanced in age, but something worn, useless, or outdated.

Nowadays we see a statement that Christians are fleeing from religiosity, that some models are outdated. However, I note that the practice of some orthodoxies can relax in some behaviors, as well as cast in others so the revelation of the Spirit is essential. , so that our walk is assertive and not slavish.

"For if the son sets you free, you will be free indeed." John 8:36

Mortification, for spiritual growth.

We affirm that we are not depersonalized, Paul shows that one of the care of the newborn in Christ must take:

It is because we do not become saints, because it is a process in the midst of spiritual battle, we do not enter into a state of perfection, but that mortification will lead us to sanctification, so we will be guided not by mental and subjective impressions or stimuli to make decisions in our lives. but the mortification of the flesh will elevate us spiritually.

“For those who bow to the flesh wonder about the things of the flesh; but those who bow to the Spirit from the things of the Spirit. 6 For the mind of the flesh is toward death, but the mind of the Spirit toward life and peace.” Romans 8:5,6

Dead flesh

It is to starve the flesh, not to nourish the earthly nature, not to opportune sin, to succumb to all the emotions that may weaken the new spiritual personality acquired by the new birth, and to highlight the fruits of the spirit so that it may advance in the realm of sin. salvation.
After conversion there is a very deep desire not to err as corresponding to the love of the Father called first love, but the bible treats us like newborn children, so we are at the mercy of mistakes and failures, and some want to put the hand in fire to know if it is truth that burns and how intense the pain, however the word tells us that sin and the old man are relentless, we can not neglect or give rise to any manifestation.

"Therefore let your earthly nature die: fornication, impurity, lascivious passion, evil desire, and covetousness, which is idolatry; 6 for these things is the wrath of God [upon the children of disobedience]. 7 Now in those same things you walked also when you lived in them. 8 But now also put off all this; anger, indignation, evil, slander, obscene language of your speaking. 9 Do not lie to one another, since you have put on the new man who is making himself full knowledge, according to the image of him who created him." Colossians 3:5,10

Mortification as protection

The biblical texts mention the human being in need of protection and in mortification protection is as cladding, dressing or cladding, armor, armor and others.
Romans have to dress like change, so is to carapace in the new life in thoughts and behavior through sanctification. This is Christ Himself in us.

"But put on the Lord Jesus Christ, and have nothing for the flesh concerning its lusts." Romans 13:14

Peter portrays mortification as a shield, for assuming our new identity we become pilgrims in strange lands subject to the enemy's attacks on hostile ground, we must not give in to the whims and feelings of our passions.

"Beloved, I exhort you, as pilgrims and strangers who are, to abstain from carnal passions, which make war with the soul, 12 keeping your course in the midst of the Gentiles, that in what they speak against you as evildoers, watching you in your good works, glorify God in the day of visitation." I Peter 2:11,12

Holy Spirit, the agent, provider, and helper in the work of mortification.

Looking at sin, we see that it is usually not only a spontaneous act but a process, just as sanctification can be gradual, regression, that is, the return to the practice of sin can be rapid.
Therefore the Holy Spirit has a fundamental role in the spiritual health of the human being, even if there is no great understanding of the free will, which is the free judgment of the person. it goes beyond human forces while temptation that is human or evil needs to be closely assisted by the Holy Spirit, who will help the believer overcome them.

"The Spirit likewise assists us in our weakness; because we cannot pray properly, but the same Spirit intercedes for us exceedingly with inexpressible moans. 27 And he that searcheth the

heart knoweth the mind of the Spirit: for according to the will of God he cometh for the saints." Romans 8:26,27

"There was no temptation to you that was not human; but God is faithful and will not allow you to be tempted beyond your might; but together with temptation he will provide you with deliverance, so that you may endure it." I Corinthians 10:13

"No one, when tempted, say, I am tempted of God; For God cannot be tempted by evil, and He does not tempt Himself. 14 On the contrary, each one is tempted by his own lust when he is attracting and seducing him. 15 Then covetousness, having conceived, bringeth forth sin; and sin, when it is finished, bringeth forth death." James 1:13,15

Fasting in mortification.

Of course the teachings show us that we must maintain a standard of holiness to smother sinful flesh, but we find in the bible something that we can use to help in this process is not a biblical or theological order but rather a suggestion and in other cases. a recommendation but who uses it has no contraindication.

That is fasting, mentioned in both the old as well as the new testament.
Fasting aims to make us abstain from something, usually food, so we guide our desires by switching from solid to spiritual food.

A deceased, breathing, anointing icon of the late times named Kenneth Hagin said he lived a fasted life, he says:

"Fasting does not change God. He is the same before during and after his fast. But fasting will change you. It will help you to be more susceptible to the Spirit of God."

The fasts mentioned in the bible have different times as well as different purposes:

One day by atonement; (Acts 27: 9)
Of three days by deliverance (Esther 4:16)
Seven days in mourning; (1 Samuel 31:13)
From fourteen days, this was involuntary (Acts 27:33)
Twenty-one day Daniel's fast and (Daniel:10:2,3)
Forty days Jesus' fast (Matthew 4:2)

Let it be very clear, it is not because you are fasting that you will be able to stir God's feelings about the sacrificial act because we are not required to suffer any kind of scourge, but if we want to have a spiritual reading it is not stuffing us that we will obtain.
That is why we cannot be extremist, that is, to live fasting or to exclude fasting from our lives, because in a victorious life like that of Christ, fasting was implicit.

Thus fasting will help in the process of mortification of the flesh, producing spiritual benefits.

The three types of fasts mentioned:

Partial: known as Daniel's abstaining from meat, wine and certain foods. (Daniel 10:2,3);
Normal: known as the fasting of Jesus, abstinence from food with fluid intake, prolonged fasting

(Matthew 4: 2).

Total: as the name implies, it was total abstinence, ie water and food (Acts 9:9).

When the Apostle Paul writes to the Galatians, he states that he no longer lives for himself, so fasting, accompanied by prayer, will bring the green revelation, for living in the flesh, that is, with human nature, will be living by faith.

"It is no longer I who live, but Christ lives in me; and this living which I now have in the flesh, I live by faith in the Son of God, who loved me and gave himself for me." Galatians 2:20

Conclusion:

Mortification is the understanding that, as Christ died crucified for our sins and revived in victory, and is the right hand of the Father, when we die in Christ in the world through the act of baptism, we want to revive too, but as we were not glorified we are at the mercy of the old man who must die every day.

Using the instrumentality of the word, with the help of the Holy Spirit, recognizing that the death of Jesus is our death, that we might rise again with him, we are enabled to live this brief time as true ambassadors of the celestial kingdom.

"For if we were united with him in the likeness of his death, surely we will be united in the likeness of his resurrection, 6 knowing this; that our old man was crucified with him, that the body of sin might be destroyed, and that we should not serve sin as slaves; 7 For he that is dead is justified from sin. 8 Now if we die with Christ, we believe that we shall also live with him." Romans 6:5,8

"For if you live according to the flesh, you walk to death; but if by the spirit you mortify the deeds of the body, you will surely live." Romans 8:13

"Always bearing in the body the death of Jesus, that his life may also be manifested in our body." II Corinthians 4:10

SANCTIFICATION

"And because iniquity shall abound, the love of many shall wax cold." Matthew 24:12
What the Bible treats as sin or perversion, today's society is turning into disease and or behavior, sanctification is a path of rapprochement with the Father, while iniquity, sin, transgression, and unholy conduct is the path diametrically opposed to holiness.
It is true that no one in himself can be perfect in this life, in which sanctification can sometimes be a gradual, long or slow work, the pursuit of sanctification must be permeated by perseverance.

"Having therefore, beloved, these promises, let us cleanse ourselves from all uncleanness, both of flesh and spirit, perfecting our holiness in the fear of God." II Corinthians 7:1

Sanctification is indispensable because it refers to our spiritual situation, which will give us the distance or closeness we have to the Throne of God.

"Follow peace with all men and holiness, without which no man shall see the Lord." Hebrews 12:14

The Portuguese language is rich in synonyms and Brazilians are often lazy for research, so when we apply the think therapy (I think that means this) or the dudeology (we deduce, whatever), we get into trouble.

At the seminar the teacher asked us what it meant: Prodigal, to answer on the spot. Beloved ones! The parable everyone knew only that no one got a definition close to its true meaning; wasteful.

Another example and the interpretation of, John 21, Jesus asks Peter, if he loves him, in our interpretation we can only see the intensity of the answers, not the question, because at its root each love quote has a weight, being comparative, disinterested love (Greek agapaõ), being friend (Greek phileõ), In sanctification happens the same, holy, holiness, sanctify, sanctifiable, sanctified and sanctification would apparently be a word with its roots, but not quite.

Notice:

In holy Hebrew is "qadosh" which means "to separate from other things." In the New Testament the Greek word for saint is "hagios", which may be separation or consecration. Now let's look at some variables in Latin:

Holy: Latin sacrare, to dedicate to God; Sacred: Latin sacratu; who has been consecrated or who has received consecration, in the initial attitude, persons and objects may be sanctifiable, consecrated, separate, holy or sanctified;

Saint: Latin *Sanctu*; established according to the law, sacred, that cannot be violated or profaned, pure, immaculate, innocent. Here the essence of God is manifest, for He is Holy, (I Peter 1:16, Leviticus 11:44,45); An exemplary individual who fully fulfills his moral and religious duties;

Holiness: Latin *sanctitate*, quality or state of saint, required by God of those who approach Him; in relation to His Majesty; divine attribute consisting of perfection;

Sanctify: Latin *sanctificare*, make holy; sanctified, who can or should be sanctified; and sanctified, who became holy; In this meaning there are holy people, things, and places; and also the name, character, power, and dignity of God must be sanctified, that is deeply revered as saints. (Buckland);

Sanctification: Latin sanctificatione, act or effect of sanctifying oneself, justification, without this it is impossible to enter into any state presented above:

"For God hath not called us to uncleanness, but to sanctification." I Thessalonians 4:7

The above words, with their respective meanings, demonstrate that one may, by misinterpretation, have a very distant understanding of what is believed. In the word game being holy is very different from being holy, for example: God is holy, cannot change.

As for us, one can already have a saintly intensity, the more separate the holier, fundamentally God's holiness requires that all who are His, or things separate for His service, relatively assume a state of holiness.

Holy; their antonym is profane, they do not go together, they do not allow themselves, they are like water and wine, salt and sugar, they have colors, smell, different taste cannot be mixed, mixed;

In the Exodus, the tabernacle gives us an idea of the process of sanctification, for the veil would have as its objective the separation between the Holy Place and the Holy of Holies (Exodus 26: 33), at the ceremony of consecration, Aaron and his sons, began with the choice of animals to sacrifice, perfect, then purification, by washing of hands, following priestly robes, sacred crown on the head, anointing with oil, then the sacrifice.

The priest sacrificed first for himself, then for the family, for the people after being certain about the purification, entering into the Holy of Holies, was a perpetual statute (Exodus 29). In the manifestation of the Lamb of God, who takes away the sin of the world, (John 1:29), the veil was torn (Matthew 27:51), so that this access would be free to the Holy of Holies in Christ Jesus, perfect and effective sacrifice (Hebrews: 9) we are led into the presence of the Father, through the reconciliation promoted by his son, (II Corinthians 5:18) God is holy, Jesus in human form was sanctified.

There is no other way, approaching without sanctification, circling with the enemy, doing what pleases you, then coming to the temple with the pretense of worship, is irrational, inconceivable !!!

Nadab and Abihu, sons of Aaron, consecrated to the office of the priesthood, with their censers, offer strange fire to the Lord and were consumed (Leviticus 10), were fit for it, but offer what God had not asked, were yes consumed by the zeal of the Lord.

"And be not conformed to this century, but be changed by the renewing of your mind, that you may experience what is the good, pleasant, and perfect will of God." Romans 12:2

How can we enter the sanctuary of the Lord (Psalm 24:3,4).

In the gospel of convenience, which we live today, holiness is low discipline, no proper value, sad mistake! Relationships shaped by mundane behavior in both dating and marriage, purity has been set aside. Not long ago the Catholic church takes a stand on pedophile and homosexual clerics, while certain so-called evangelical churches are ordaining and being ministered by people who are declared homosexuals (I Corinthians 6:9). can come to His knowledge. But zeal for the word is imperative, when it is said to be more prudent in the children of darkness than in light! (Luke 16: 8) Which side are we on?

Starting with our body, we will find:

“Do you not know that you are God's sanctuary, and that the Spirit of God dwells in you?”

"If anyone destroys the sanctuary of God, God will destroy him; For it is the sanctuary of God, which you are, that is holy." I Corinthians 3

In holiness we are directed to a holy, worthy course, as we go out into the ways of life the mark of Christ must be on our face, if we have been washed in the blood of the lamb, no stain is accepted, pure in action, in walking, in living:

"Live above all in a manner worthy of the gospel of Christ..." Philippians 1:27a

Consciousness and lawfulness can bring difficulties in the process of sanctification, for in some cases what is lawful or what suits me (I Corinthians 10:23) may tarnish the aspect of holiness, so we have been chosen to be holy and blameless. before him, the Holy One of Israel (Ephesians 1:4).

In sanctification there is no coexistence or tolerance for sin, not that a Christian does not sin, but if he sins, he must admit his errors and purge them, with due forgiveness.

"Do not be yoked together with unbelievers; For what society can there be between justice and iniquity? Or what communion between light and darkness? 15 What harmony between Christ and the Evil One? Or what union between the believer and the unbeliever? 16 What connection is there between the sanctuary of God and idols? For we are the living sanctuary of God, as he himself said, I will dwell and walk among them; I will be their God, and they will be my people. 17 Therefore depart from their midst, and separate yourselves, and I will receive you." II Corinthians 6:14,17

Sanctification in the Old Testament.

Old Testament sanctification is associated with the idea of purity; of separation; shine and cut.

Beginning with Abram the patriarch the process of sanctification takes place in the order of departure from the midst of his kin, that is, distancing was separation, and cutting was with the idolatrous bonds practiced by the Chaldeans. To separate was to sanctify.

"Now the Lord said to Abram; Come out of your land from your kindred and from your father's house and go to the land that I will show you: 2 I will make you a great nation, and I will bless you, and thank your name. Be a blessing!" Genesis 12:1,2

Thus marking in Abram the process of sanctification by the first unilateral theocratic covenant of the Father, for it is He who makes the promise.

A second mark of sanctification that we can cite as to brightness is the call of Moses, for we see God's care from his birth, but when he goes up the mountain to receive the commandment tablets, he is separated from the people, fasting, when he goes down the people could not look at her face because she glowed.

"When Moses came down from Mount Sinai, holding the two tablets of the Testimony in his hand, even as he came down from the mount, Moses did not know that the skin of his face shone after God had spoken to him. 30 And when Aaron and all the children of Israel looked unto Moses, behold, the skin of his face shone; and they feared to come unto him." Exodus 34:29,30

Therefore sanctification in Moses was marked by communion with God and seen by all as a sign on his face.

The people of Israel themselves were chosen to be a holy people, separated with a different religious, moral and ethical behavior from all existing nations.

In religious practice the Father passes on information, rules regarding the worship of his celebration, and the utensils to be used. People and utensils were separated for the service of worship.

"Therefore, sanctify yourselves and be holy, for I am the LORD your God. 8Keep my statutes and fulfill them. I am the LORD that sanctify you." Leviticus 20:7,8

Thus in the Old Testament it is evident that persons were set apart, for a special commission, for the priesthood, for the prophetic, and for the monarchical exercise, also consecrated utensils that could not be used for other purposes.

Sanctification in the New Testament.

In the New Testament sanctification, it is used to describe a state of behavior that does not neglect the ethical, moral and religious question.

Hagios describes sanctification as separation from the practice of sin and then as consecration to the service of the celestial kingdom.

Sanctification as well as justification, regeneration, adoption occurs initially at the new birth. Therefore it begins in conversion and continues until glorification. Then we may live in a state of eternal holiness in Christ.

The initial step:

When conjugated the verb sanctify in the perfect past tense composed "I have sanctified"

The Bible shows us that we have already been sanctified in Jesus, but moves on to something future.

That is the second step the so-called progressive step:

"To the church of God which is in Corinth, to the sanctified in Christ Jesus, called to be saints, with all that call on the name of our Lord Jesus Christ, their Lord and ours everywhere." I Corinthians 1:2

In the progressive stage, the same apostle brings the need that, besides being a complete work, he must reach the three elements of human composition: body, soul and spirit.

"And the God of peace himself sanctify you in all things; and let your spirit, soul, and body be preserved whole and blameless at the coming of our Lord Jesus Christ." I Thessalonians 5:23

Recalling that the need to sanctify ourselves is because we are guilty of the human degradation generated by sinful practice, which will be penalized because of human disobedience toward the Father.

This penalty is withdrawn only by the justification advanced in Christ as the concept of justification thus presented.

Degradation or corruption can only be dealt with by sanctification, for it is a cleansing work, restoring fellowship with God in Christ, who, innocent by justification, begin to develop spiritually in righteousness by the word and the help of the Holy Spirit.

"However, we must always give thanks to God for you, the Lord's beloved brothers, because God has chosen you from the beginning for salvation through the sanctification of the Spirit and faith in the truth." II Thessalonians 2:13

The holy state is required of all, for sanctification, which is the process of gradual improvement that seeks to approach the divine character, must be sought with care.

"Therefore be perfect as your heavenly Father is perfect." Matthew 5:48

"For it is written, Be holy, because I am holy." I Peter 1:16

The Sanctification of Human Trichotomy

The first element that receives sanctification is the Human Spirit, for when Adam sinned it was the cardinal spirit of communion with God. When we recognize Jesus as savior our Spirit is reconnected with the Father, which is the process of regeneration, a concept already presented with his name.

"Jesus answered, Verily, verily, I say unto you, he that is not born of water and the Spirit cannot enter into the kingdom of God. 6 What is born of the flesh is flesh; and what is born of the Spirit is spirit. 7 No wonder I say, you must be born again." John 3:5,7

The second element is the Soul, as we are not depersonalized, the soul or psyche, which is the seat of our emotions and wills, must be restored.

One mistake of recent times is exactly in the matter of the soul, for many believe that if the Spirit has been regenerated the soul is regenerated; but it must be restored.

"And be not conformed to this century, but be changed by the renewing of your mind, that you may experience what is the good, pleasant, and perfect will of God." Romans 12:2

An analogy that Jesus presents is in the parable of wine. Mentioning a new message as new wine and the restored human being as a new wineskin (Matthew 9:17).

The third is the body, this is an agent who delights in sin, for the sensations and pleasure of sin is in the body:

"Let each one of you abstain from prostitution; 4 Let every one of you know how to possess his own body in sanctification and honor, 5 not with desire for lewdness, as Gentiles that know not God; 6 And let no one offend or deceive his brother in this matter; for the Lord, against all these things, as we warned you before, and plainly testified, is the avenger, 7 for God hath not called us to impurity, but to sanctification." I Thessalonians: 4:3,7

The soul acts as the guide, because if it bends to the Spirit, it wants the assurance of salvation that is through sanctification, while if it bends to the body, it will feed on corruption.

"I beseech you therefore, brethren, by the mercies of God, to present your body as a living sacrifice, holy and pleasing to God, which is your rational worship." Romans 12:1

That said, we have to use the body for sanctification, in fear of God.

"Therefore, having such promises, beloved, let us cleanse ourselves from all uncleanness of both flesh and spirit, perfecting our holiness in the fear of God." II Corinthians 7:1

Examples of holiness in the New Testament

Who gets top marks, the "hors concours" is the Lord Jesus, stripped of his glory, showed the world what holiness is possible.

And as much as you peer into the concept of holiness, it is not exhausted, for it transcends.

Knowing that sanctification is a complete work that does not fall within a certain limit of behavior or concept, I highlight an element of three apostles who left a legacy in teaching and witness.

In the Apostle Paul, evangelist, missionary, teacher etc.:

The element is suffering, the mark of his holiness in the suffering he experienced, produced joy because he understood that this was answering his call. After persecuting the Christians, he was now the persecuted.

"But the Lord said unto him, Go, for this is an instrument chosen for me, to bear my name before the Gentiles and kings, and before the children of Israel; 16 For I will show you how much it matters to you to suffer for my name." Acts 9:15,16

"Are they ministers of Christ?" (I speak as outside myself.) I even more: in works, much more; much more in prisons; in stripes, without measure; in danger of death often. 24 Five times I received from the Jews a quarantine of whips minus one; 25 I was struck three times with rods; once stoned; in wreck three times; one night and one day I spent in the whirlwind of the sea; 26 on journeys often; river hazards, robber hazards, patrician hazards; in danger among Gentiles, in danger in the city; in dangers in the desert, in dangers in the sea, in dangers among false brethren; 27 in labor and fatigue, in watchings often; in hunger and thirst, in fasts often; in cold

and nakedness." II Corinthians 11:23,27

In the Apostle Peter, evangelist, prophet and visionary.

The element of holiness, was in the anointing for miracles, more than once to perform the miracle he entered the dimensional faith, his holiness entered the supernatural, who heals with the shadow of his body? Just Peter.

"To the point that they may take the sick to the streets and put them on beds and stretchers, so that, as Peter passed by, at least his shadow would fall on some of them." Acts 5:15

In the Apostle John the prophet.

The element of holiness was in love in the capacity of separation to receive the supernatural. Bringing in a unique way the revelation of the future to the present.

"Revelation of Jesus Christ, which God gave unto him to show unto his servants the things which must shortly come to pass, and which he, sending through his angel, notified to his servant John, 2 which attested to the word of God and the testimony of Jesus Christ as to all that he saw." Revelation 1:1,2

The fruit of sanctification

The Apostle Paul, quoted by Peter says that he has things that are hard to understand, (II Peter 3:16). Always in Paul's wordplay, which bluntly discusses how much we are free from sin, he puts in check our Free then, when he becomes servants, he does not exercise his own will, but in this way we become productive in the sense of sanctification; and as a consequent prize is to receive eternal life.

"But now being delivered from sin, made servants of God, ye have your fruit unto sanctification, and finally to everlasting life." Romans 6:22

GLORIFICATION

Finally we come to the last concept to be presented in the order of salvation, of course because it is something future not yet lived, what we have are many speculations.
Glorification is the final state of all saved in Christ. As broadly described in the concepts of justification, adoption, regeneration, and sanctification which is the initial or transformative state of the individual now made a child of God, we will receive through glorification all the rewards if any. we can say so, by obedience and perseverance in the way of faith.
Thus glorification will be to live in a state of glory, splendor, honor, and respect, which the Lord God will bring to all his own.

"For I am sure that the sufferings of the present time cannot be compared with the glory to be revealed in us" Romans 8:18

Glorification; Action of glorifying; ascension to eternal glory, elevation of the righteous, and exaltation.

Glory: Splendor, brilliance, honor, respect and majesty.

Subjective concept of glory: Optical phenomenon on the observer's shadow, an effect that occurs when light tunneling, when light rays pass through the air into water droplets, or antelium, which is the light reflected from the sun on the opposite side to this star.
This concept is interesting because the brightness of a star the sun is reflected in a drop of water, is something tangible can be seen, but intense. So what will the reflection of the mighty God look like in a person?

Biblical concept of glory:

In the old testament. Glory is Kabod. We see in the texts that glory had a direct connotation with the presence of God; Whether behind the rock where Moses stood, in the pillar of smoke in the tabernacle, fire and shadow in the wilderness walk, means assistance and protection with his people, later his presence was reflected in the ark of the covenant where the ark was there. the presence of God.

The glory of God was also understood as his total and unrestricted magnificence of his presence in salvation, judgment as well as in his theophany (whether by the Father or the son).

A text from 1 Samuel shows that with the taking of the ark the glory of the Lord was cut off from Israel generating judgment and death.

"But he called the boy Ichabod, saying; The glory of Israel is gone. This she said; for the ark of God was taken, and because of her father in law, and her husband." I Samuel 5:21

This woman's statement was, "Where is the glory?" Or "We are without glory!" So if for the Jews it was the Father's presence. The text means, "Where is this God?"
It is true that God did not abandon them, for He was disciplining them with the future events narrated in this same book.

Another term used for God's dwelling or presence was from the Hebrew: shkn "dwelling" (shekinah). Understood as the living glory of God.

So what we see in the Old Testament about God's glory, basically was when His presence was revealed.

In the New Testament shekinah is also present.
"Yet he spake when a bright cloud enveloped them; and behold. From the cloud came a voice saying, This is my beloved Son, in whom I am well pleased; I have heard him.
" Matthew 17:5

But the verb Kabod is no longer used to use the term "Doxa" which becomes more comprehensive and relative, as it reaches other meanings: as to express the presence of the Father, a future position, a crown symbolizing conquest. (I Peter 5:4) and worship God through worship that also reveals his glory.

Dox (a) means: Glory, belief or opinion, where doxology arises, the generally rhythmic liturgical formula of praise to God, and doxomania = dox (o) + mania: passion to acquire glory.

GLORIFICATION:

It is the ultimate perfection and ultimate perfection that will reach human trichotomy. The spirit will receive eternity, returning to the initial state for which it was created, that is to the realm of the whole being; the soul the incorruptibility will cease to be susceptible to the desires and sensations experienced today and the body the immortality will assume a new composition, which possibly our source of energy, or its absorption will be otherwise. Because the natural body will become spiritual.

"For indeed those in this tabernacle groan in distress, not because we would be stripped, but clothed, that the mortal may be absorbed in life." II Corinthians 5:4

"For so is the resurrection of the dead. The body is sown in corruption, it is raised in incorruption. Sow in dishonor, rise in glory. 43 It is sown in weakness, it is raised in power.44 It is sown in the natural body, it resurrects the spiritual body. If there is a natural body, there is also a spiritual body.45 For thus it is written: The first man, Adam was made a living soul. The last Adam, however, is a life-giving spirit. 46 But it is not the spiritual first, but the natural; then the spiritual." I Corinthians 15:42,46

An addendum to the state we are about to receive glorification is that:

• One will be glorified in life;
• Another will be glorified when he is dead.

The first guarantee of his glorification is to be caught in the rapture of the sanctified church.
The second is to have experienced the first death with its name listed in the book of life.

"Behold, I tell you a mystery; We will not all sleep, but we will all be transformed in a moment, in the twinkling of an eye, as the last trumpet resounds. The trumpet will sound, the dead will be raised incorruptible, and we will be changed. 53 For this corruptible body must put on incorruption, and the mortal body put on immortality. 54 And when this corruptible body put on incorruption, and the mortal put on immortality, then the word that is written shall be fulfilled: Death was swallowed up by victory." I Corinthians 15:51,54

Therefore glorification is the final stage of our redemption.

"For if we believe that Jesus died and rose again, so God through Jesus will bring those who sleep with him. 15 And we have told you this by the word of the LORD; we who are alive, who remain until the coming of the Lord, will not precede those who sleep. 16 For the Lord Himself, having given His word of command, and heard the voice of the archangel, and the trumpet of God shall sound, shall come down from heaven, and the dead in Christ shall rise first; 17 Then we the living who are left shall be caught up together with them in the clouds to meet the Lord in the air, and we shall be with the Lord forever." I Thessalonians 4:14,17

Soon there is the resurrection of all who have experienced death, but Christ makes it clear that some are for victory and others for their just punishment.

"Marvel not at this, for the hour is coming when all who are in graves shall hear his voice, and shall go forth; 29 those who have done good for the resurrection of life; and those who have done evil for the resurrection of judgment." John 5:28,29

As well as our justification and sanctification are confirmed in the act of glorification.

"Now to him that is mighty to stumble over you, and to present you with joy, without spot before his glory." Jude 24

Purpose of glorification.

If Adam and Eve had not sinned what would be the man state? But they have sinned and the result is there! Questions that are only answered by divine attributes.

So what we are dealing with is the post fall results and expectations, so we have hope in the Old Testament about future human glorification, we have the believer's victory amid the tribulations guaranteed by sanctification and the overcomers of the great tribulation,

The first point was the hope of the ancients in the remission of the soul, as they did not know Jesus, certainly they expected in Jehovah in all their manifestations such as:

Jehovah-Tsidkenu "In his days Judah shall be saved, and Israel shall dwell safely; This shall be his name, and he shall be called, Lord, our righteousness." Jeremiah 23,6

"But God will redeem my soul from the power of death, for he will take me unto himself." Psalms 49:15

The second already widely appreciated in the previous concepts:

"Be faithful unto death, and I will give you the crown of life." Revelation 2:10b.

And the third is due to his declaration of faith and persistence in the midst of great tribulation.

"I said to him, My Lord, you know. He then said unto me, These are they that come out of the great tribulation, washed their garments, and made them white in the blood of the Lamb."

Revelation 7:14

Therefore the purpose of glorification as described by John, in the vision of the glorified, (Revelation 7:9,17). is to show that what is promised will be fulfilled, glorification is the reward for faithfulness, and the chief come to purpose by which we were created to "Serve and worship God."

Results of glorification.

The deepest result of glorification is that we have a body like Christ's.
Soon, we entered into lands little known and studied by Christians, for lack of revelation or simple interests.

"This I say, brethren, that flesh and blood cannot inherit the kingdom of God, nor corruption inherit incorruption." I Corinthians 15:50

We see people preoccupied with deciphering the apocalypse, looking for predictions about the future, nothing wrong with what they are doing, but when we really lack elementary knowledge and information at the present time.

The Bible shows that there is no possibility of dwelling in the heavens as we are today, but that the three persons testify in heaven, and that the Son ascended into heaven as he lived on earth, being recognized in heaven by bodily form,

What we see is that his body was glorified and for that, a high price was paid: his blood.

Thus the sense of Jesus' glorification began with the emptying of his blood on the cross and not a drop of blood, for it was the full price for the ransom of our lives. Because in the Old Testament it shows that life is in the blood, the blood is gone, the life is over!

"For there are three that bear witness [in heaven: the Father, the Word, and the Holy Ghost; and these three are one. 8 And three are they that bear witness to the earth]: the Spirit, the water, and the blood, and the three are unanimous not only in purpose." I John 5:7

"Therefore the life of all flesh is its blood; therefore I have said to the children of Israel; You shall not eat the blood of any flesh, for the life of all flesh is its blood." Leviticus 17:14a

We will assume a heavenly but not disfigured image; every downfall of our bodies will be extinguished, for the texts carry the claim that we will be Christlike.

When Jesus asks to be touched after the resurrection, they show that the spirit has no flesh and bones. And He had!

We also see the ability to move from place to place and transpose matter as it has passed through the wall.

"See my hands and my feet, that I am myself; grope me and see, for a spirit has neither flesh nor bone, as ye see that I have." Luke 24:39

The skills that the glorified will have will leave any ufological sight terrified, for:

Time, space, gravity and mass will be easily mastered.

"And he was transfigured before them; his face shone like the sun, and his raiment became white as the light." Matthew 17:2

Today food and sleep are necessary for our survival, after glorified the indications, show that we will feed, and this food will be transformed into pure energy, as for sleep we will no longer sleep, for we will be before the Father and the Son, beholding them the face.

"Jesus came, took the bread, and gave them, and the fish also." John 21:13

"There will never be any curse again. In it will be the throne of God and the Lamb. His servants shall serve him; 4 they shall behold his face, and his name is on his forehead. 5 Then there will be no night, and they need no light of light, nor sunlight, for the Lord God will shine upon him, and they shall reign for ever and ever." Revelation: 22:3,5

In creation God formed man from clay and breathed into his nostrils into a living soul (Genesis: 2; 7), which means that in man was placed the qualities of life that form his character or essence, which were degraded. in the fall.

In glorification, we observe that the one who takes control of the body and the decisions is the Spirit, which can be understood as a fusion of these two elements: body and spirit.

"Natural body is sown, spiritual body resurrected. If there is a natural body, there is also a spiritual body.45 For thus it is written: The first man, Adam was made a living soul. The last Adam, however, is a life-giving spirit. 46 But it is not the spiritual first, but the natural; then the spiritual.47 The first man, formed from the earth, is earthly; The second man is from heaven. 48 As was the first man, the earthy, so are the other men of the earth; and as is the heavenly man, so are the heavenly, 49And as we have brought the image of the earthly, we must also bear the image of the heavenly." I Corinthians 15:44,49

Paul reports meeting a man who went to heaven and who saw extraordinary things, we understand that he was speaking of himself, so when he teaches about our heavenly abode and the new composition of our eternal existence he knew what he was talking about.

When we teach from those who have mastery, motivating action takes on new forms, and the Apostle categorically motivates us, saying that what we have to pass the fragility of our body, the tribulations nothing at all compares with what lies ahead.

The metaphor that this servant presents is the difference of a nomadic dwelling, since there is no permanent dwelling, and the tents are easily dismantled to continue other paths, uncertainties and resistance in these dwellings is a constant. Thus he states when our earthly abode undoing yes we will receive a building, solid and eternal.

"We know that if our earthly house of this tabernacle were dissolved, we have a building from God, a house not made with hands, eternal in heaven. 2 And therefore in this tabernacle we groan, longing to be clothed with our heavenly habitation;" II Corinthians 5:1,2

Time of glorification.

Our homesick Myles Munroe preached that all God begins is because He has already finished. Thus Jesus began the process of glorification but His glory will be seen on earth when He returns to take the church with Him.

This time of glorification begins at the Rapture and where does it end?

A good question to ask yourself in eternity!

"Father, my will is that where I am, may those who have given me also be with me, that they may see my glory which thou hast bestowed upon me, because thou hast loved me before the foundation of the world." John 17:24

"Then we the living who are left shall be caught up together with them in the clouds to meet the Lord in the air, and thus we shall be with the Lord forever." I Thessalonians 4:17

We have come to the end of the concepts of the order of salvation, reiterating that the content of this material is not intended to exhaust the subject but to situate our position as children of the Most High. Paulo.

Where there is a foreordination, a calling, justification, and finally glorification.

"And whom He predestined, these He also called; and whom he called, he also justified; and whom He justified, them He also glorified." Romans 8:30

CONCLUSION

In addition to the concepts of the four lines of the order of salvation we find twenty three, of these twelve are the most accepted and in this material were commented eleven, leaving out the predestination, because we believe that these concepts, as I have already witnessed, leads to uncertainties as to salvation of people and relativization when the needy discipline is needed.

Leaving unambiguous interpretations leading many of its adherents to make grotesque mistakes, we accept part of this concept, there is no rejection completely, just some care about the zeal of the word.

We know that many Armenianists have no difficulty accepting it, for we firmly believe that this concept is as foreordination, not predestination as a fait accompli.

The conceptual steps are dogmatically defined for designating the work of the Holy Spirit in the process of salvation as a whole. Therefore, discussing each concept positions us at what moment each of these concepts is situated, either instantaneously or progressively, understanding the objectivity or exclusivity of God in each of these steps.

Therefore, when we obey Jesus' imperative command in Matthew 28, we become collaborators in the process of salvation to all who listen to this message.

What is the reward of this work? Many have had a lifetime devoted to the gospel, others a short time, the salary itself and the same for all, regardless of how much time we devote to this service or ministry.

Explained in the parable of the workers in the vineyard in Matthew:

"When the first came, they thought they would receive more; but these also received one denarius each. 11 But when they had received him, they murmured against the master of the house, 12 saying, The latter worked only one hour; But you have made them equal to us, who endure the fatigue and the heat of the day. 13 But the landlord answered and said to one of them, Friend, I do not wrong thee; Didn't you combine a denarius? 14 Take what is yours and go; for I want to give the latter as much as you." Matthew 20:10,14

Another question is how the human being will come to the knowledge of salvation, because, well, we mentioned that the patriarchs expected salvation so there is a divine criterion for this, to those born in the New Testament the criterion is set forth in the gospels, and certainly who born in the post-tribulation period, of course they were not left out of this plan.
The plan and work is complete in order to arrive at the heavenly abode, whether by the rapture, or by the visitation of death and later judgment.

"Repent therefore, and be converted, that your sins may be blotted out, 20 so that from the presence of the Lord may come times of refreshing, and that he may send forth the Christ whom he hath appointed, Jesus, 21 to whom heaven must receive until the time of the restoration of all things, which God hath spoken by the mouth of his holy prophets from ancient times." Acts 3:19,21

In this material, it can not be said that it is only didactic, as it has instructions and comments, experiences of various orders. The purpose is clear: to be able to help, lovers of Bible studies, all forms of visions that need a specific text, according to the need that the moment in the discipleship requires.

Prayers and tears are known in heaven, distressing moments lived, that make us experienced and hopeful about the promises made.
One thing I learned:
Once a test or tribulation is passed, if approved, another level of proof will come, knowing that the purpose is not reprobation, but experience.
The psalms say, Even if your father and your mother forsake you, yet the Lord does not forsake you (Psalms 27:10).
Paul warns us: firm and constant in the Lord's promises.

"Therefore, my beloved brethren; stand firm and unshaken, and abound always in the work of the Lord; knowing that in the Lord your work is not in vain." I Corinthians 15:58

I close with the sincere wish that all who have contact with this writing will receive salvation; and quote:

"Then I heard a loud voice from the throne saying, Behold, the tabernacle of God with men. God will dwell with him. They will be God's people, and God Himself will be with him. 4 And all tears shall be wiped from their eyes, and death shall be no more; there shall be no mourning, nor weeping, nor pain; for the first things are passed away. 5 And he that sitteth on the throne said, Behold, I make all things new. And he said, Write, because these words are faithful and true. 6 And he said unto me, Everything is done. I am Alpha and Omega, the Beginning and the End. I who thirst will give freely of the fountain of the water of life. 7 The victor will inherit these things, and I will be his God, and he will be my son." Revelation 21:3,7

BIBLIOGRAPHY

Bible Study of Prophecy: Publisher Acts and Bible Society of Brazil.
Study Bible Macarthur; Bible Society of Brazil.
Blogs, various.
Buckland; Universal biblical dictionary;
Aurélio dictionaries online.
Online Dictionary, Dictionaries Michaelis;
Free Bible Studies, Google
Little Bible Encyclopedia, Orlando Boyer, Assemblies of God Institutes.
Google searches.
Wikipedia, The Free Encyclopedia,

When we enter Christianity, we find that in a simplified way for some, who do not accept criticism or disagreement, under the affirmation of our faith that blindly must be obeyed and ready.

Yet even within this faith that is monotheistic that believes in one God. We see distortions and childishness being practiced.

We find apparently an idea of a God who: Creates a man gives him a law called free will, and if he did not correspond to him, he would show him another project called redemption that would be obtained strictly by Faith.

When we then come across lines of interpretation of the real concept of this faith, then questions arise: how and why of certain liturgies and affirmations of what to believe, thinking of this we go to a logical situation:

Is there a chronological or even logical order of this faith?

Then we find four concrete lines that were grounded in the early days of Christianity, which is ORDER SALVATIS (ORDO SALUTIS) conceptualized and propagated by Roman Catholicism, Lutheranism, Arminianism, and Calvinism.

With different views on the same faith each doctrinal current claims to be its position. the correct, or at least true to what the sacred scriptures reveal to us, yet right now we are having a hard time with what goes on as theological grounding.

Some put voracious rules making it difficult for people thirsting for salvation, others put ease relativizing this same rule of salvation. But nothing is more logical than to observe what the sound doctrine tells us.

Regardless of the interpretations one has, the identified chronology is from the CALL by the Lutheran concept. The call can be understood as; Jesus' presentation of his acceptance or conversion. Culminating with GLORIFICATION by the Arminian and Calvinist concepts. That is the final state of the believer in Jesus.

Pastor Selito Carlos Meira, was separated to pastoral ministry in 1988, Married to Pastor RUTH M. F. MEIRA, has two children Gabriel and Isabel. Pastor several churches in Brazil, is Senior Pastor and President of the Gospel Community(IGREJA COMUNIDADE DO EVANGLEHO) Based in Cascavel- Parana state- Brazil. Lived in Italy and currently resides in the England.

Printed by Books on Demand GmbH, Norderstedt / Germany